ISBN: 9781980486404

Fight Back Manual

Last Bet Strategies for Survival of our Western Civilization

Pierre A. Kandorfer, Ph.D.

Dedicated to the three women in my life
I love and cherish most:

My wife Helga Kandorfer
My daughter Michelle Dominique Nolting
My granddaughter Diana Maria Nolting

Chapter Overview

"Our Judeo-Christian heritage is the foundation of our great republic. If we lose that, we lose the essence of who we are."
(Lt. Col. Allen West)

God help us!

Our world appears to be totally upside down. We can't get rid of the impression that "everything is lost" already. More and more Constitution-loving and traditionally, family-oriented Americans get the feeling that praying is the only thing left.

However, we can't give up. Self-pity doesn't help anyone. Let's resist the Marxist takeover of our country. Let's convey our moral courage and sense our sacred obligation to defend our civilization.

"Our last bet" is at the same time "our only bet." It's all encouraging hope, vision, spirituality and energy we can synergize. It is our primary and highest priority for the rest of our lives.

It only remains our last bet if we fail, but failure is not an option while we are trying to rescue our culture.

As much as we sometimes feel that praying is the only thing left, we also must take action. God will help us, but only if we start helping ourselves.

You don't win if you don't fight.

We won't lose, at least not without a fight!

What is at stake for us?

The basis of our Judeo-Christian civilization, our democracy, personal freedoms and rights are reflected in our Constitution and our Bill of Rights.

According to Charles N. Quigley (Center for Civic Education), constitutional democracy is the antithesis of arbitrary rule. It is democracy characterized by:

1. **Popular sovereignty**
   The people are the ultimate source of the authority of the government, which derives its right to govern from their consent.

2. **Majority rule and minority rights**
   Although "the majority rules," the fundamental rights of individuals in the minority are protected.

3. **Limited government**
   The powers of government are limited by law and a written or unwritten constitution, which those in power obey.

4. **Institutional and procedural limitations of powers**
   There are certain institutional and procedural devices, which limit the powers of government. These may include:

5. **Separated and shared powers**
   Powers are separated among different agencies or branches of government. Each agency or branch has primary responsibility for certain functions such as legislative, executive, and judicial functions. However, each branch also shares these functions with the other branches.

6. **Checks and balances**
   Different agencies or branches of government
   have adequate power to check the powers of other
   branches. Checks and balances may include the
   power of judicial review, the power of courts to
   declare actions of other branches of government to
   be contrary to the constitution and therefore null
   and void.

7. **Due process of law**
   Individual rights to life, liberty and property are
   protected by the guarantee of due process of law.

8. **Leadership succession through elections**
   Elections ensure that key positions in government
   will be contested at periodic intervals and that the
   transfer of governmental authority is accomplished
   in a peaceful and orderly process.

Values worth defending

First of all, we must define values we intend to defend. There are different types of values:

Social values

Social values include aspects such as freedom, peace, equality, honesty and fairness.

1. Honesty
2. Generosity
3. Respectfulness
4. Courteous
5. Fairness
6. Caring for the community

Political values

Political values depend mainly on your worldview and should include opinions on how to run the government - or which laws are appropriate and must be enforced.

1. Belief in American exceptionalism, based on our unique Constitution
2. Belief in free-market capitalism and private ownership of property
3. Patriotism
4. Viewing and treating everybody equally, independently of ethnicity, race or religion
5. Open-mindedness
6. Respect for our laws
7. Working hard for success

Religious values

Following the Ten Commandments, Christian values demand specific behaviours such as:

1. Compassion for people in need
2. Treating everybody the way you want to be treated
3. Growing and learning spiritually and intellectually
4. Displaying modesty in your relations and other parts of your life
5. Respectful and non-violent interaction with other people

Work values

Work values affect your attitude towards your job, finances and how you raise and educate your kids.

1. Trying to do always best at work
2. Promoting teamwork
3. Saving a portion of your income for the rainy days
4. Searching for opportunities to express your values, ideas and creativity
5. Pride of your achievements
6. Placing education on the top of your priority list
7. Awareness of the fact, which role plays your job in the society
8. Treating your customers and other people in a respectful way

Moral values

Moral values of a Christian worldview are the foundation of our lives. They determine what we consider right or wrong and how we raise and teach our children. Here are some general examples:

1. Honesty
2. Trustworthiness
3. Patience
4. Responsibility
5. Accountability

6. Never give up
7. Contribution to goodness

Recreational values

Recreation is an important part of family life. It refers to all aspects of "fun and play" and contributes to creating social skills, common memories, family closeness and learning opportunities.

1. Spending quality time together as a family
2. Taking family vacations
3. Encouraging family members to pursue specific interests
4. Creating unstructured play time
5. Organizing family game nights

Determine your core family values

Sometimes it is very useful to talk to all other family members and determine the most important values you want to pursue.

1. Determine your core values
2. Create a distinctively positive family culture
3. Consider writing a mission statement of your family
4. Talk to each other as often as possible
5. Allow everybody to think or rethink all ideas discussed in any brainstorming
6. Stick to major ideas
7. Write down all important aspects such as checklist, scheduling or meeting plans in order to enhance your quality time together

What can we learn?

1. Do what you think and think what you do

2. Always be honest
3. Always be authentic with no exception
4. Show your love every single day
5. Consider all consequences before you act
6. Follow the Christian worldview
7. Discuss and defend traditional values when confronted by "contemporary" values
8. Spend quality time with your family without disregarding your personal interests
9. Live in accordance with your values, don't just talk about them
10. Treat everybody with compassion and respect
11. Do your best and let God do the rest
12. Always continue to learn
13. Celebrate success
14. Use your money to "do" something – rather than "buying" something
15. Don't always act only on your current feeling
16. Don't be impatient and don't expect everything to be done immediately
17. See the "big picture" and everything as a whole and don't stick on minor problems
18. Listen to other people and view everything from different angles and viewpoints
19. Evaluate your strategies
20. Get rid of relationships hurting you or your family

How to fight the culture war

How to promote our constitutional principles?

1. Read thoroughly the US Constitution and the Declaration of Independence.
2. Try to understand it completely.
3. Discuss it with your family, friends, acquaintances and colleagues.
4. Monitor our public life in order to find out where our constitutional principles are violated.
5. Don't accept any violations of our constitutional rights. The tiniest beginning might one day lead to a total loss of our basic human rights such as free speech and others.
6. Engage any offender in any way appropriate. This can start with a small personal talk to a politician, teacher or freedom-hating activist, but can develop to a public discussion, media action or demonstration.
7. Always know the Constitution and the Bill of Rights thoroughly ahead of any kind of dispute and be prepared for any kind of challenge.
8. Contact Constitution-defending organizations and evaluate their approach. Try to establish some kind of strategic cooperation and/or support them.
9. Research, which politicians, groups and organizations attempt to destroy our Constitution and confront them.
10. Use social media to spread your message.

How can we save our schools and colleges?

Except Marxist sympathizers, nobody doubts that our educational system presents an unbearable crisis and terrible danger for the future of our society. Exploding cost, failing grades, anti-American and anti-Christian propaganda reveal that we must be doing something dreadfully wrong in our schools and colleges. It is worse than you think!

While our main-stream media rarely criticize our public education system, Conservapedia collected some of the most critical and totally unacceptable facts:

1. 30% of public school students fail to graduate
2. 40% of minorities fail to graduate
3. 70% of leave high school unqualified to enter a 4-year college
4. 77% of students between 8th and 12th grade use illicit drugs
5. 50% of viable public high school teenager pregnancies end in abortions
6. 20% of students are involved in dangerous binge drinking
7. 10% of our public high schools have a homosexual club
8. 10% of students have mental health problems
9. 160,000 miss school daily

Public schools in the US employ several million people, spend over four hundred billion dollars per year – this is over 10,000 per student. At the same time, many schools in America do the following:

1. Censor free speech
2. Outlaw classroom prayer
3. Outlaw the Bible on campus and refuse any kind of Judeo-Christian values and morals in schools and colleges.
4. Promote the Marxist worldview
5. Promote a radical environmental agenda
6. Promote homosexual indoctrination
7. Object to virtually everything that represents traditional American values.

Our educational institutions are in the process of a total "reprogramming" of our children away from morals and values expressed in the Ten Commandments.

While gay clubs or Muslim organizations are welcome in many schools, Bible clubs or Pro-Life gatherings are rarely acceptable. What is typical in many US high schools today?

1. Banning of the US flag on school campus
2. Forbidding the Pledge of Allegiance on campus
3. Suspension of students with a Bible found in their school locker, while the Communist Manifesto is "welcome education tool"
4. Requests for grater "condom availability" are often granted
5. School invitations to gay bars are acceptable
6. Welcoming of all gay, lesbian or transgender ideas on campus
7. Cross-dressing of boys and girls are tolerable
8. Labeling Christians as "oppressors"
9. Mandatory Arabic classes are increasing
10. Mandatory citing of "Five Pillars of Islam" in the class
11. Mandatory visits and Muslim praying in Mosques
12. Preferential treatment of Muslim students

The total indoctrination of school children with a Marxist worldview is often called "the necessary character education." This is frighteningly like the "re-education" camps communists did in Stalin's Gulags and North Vietnamese, North Korean or Chinese prison camps.

How can we get started?

1. Educate yourself about the state of our education in all phases from kindergarten to the graduate school.

2. Define all major obstacles such as Teacher's Union.
3. Create a resistance plan.
4. Focus on like-minded parents and other people.
5. Establish a formal or informal action group.
6. Consider ballot measures to advance your educational demands.
7. Support politicians who demand the elimination of the Dept. of Education and shifting all educational measures to states.
8. Confront schools, administrators, teachers, principals and other institutions involved with specific demands.
9. Educate yourself about the Evolution theory and Bible-based Creationism.
10. Prove that there is no proof for the atheist-promoted Darwin's evolution theory. One of thousands of facts on your side: If life "evolved" from nothing to bacteria and then to all kinds of living creatures like a human being, why haven't we found one single fossil example of a transitional life form (i. e. between a fish and a bird)?
11. Demand to at least add Creationism to the current school curriculum.
12. Force educators to stop attacking American exceptionalism.
13. Engage teachers who slander the free-market-society and capitalism.
14. Fight schools promoting the Marxism-style glorification of a big government.

How to learn from successful experience

As Chuck Norris emphasizes, there are some ways to improve our education by changing the deeply screwed worldview imbalances in our schools. Many conservative parents, educators and organizations have launched successful counter-measures and started changing our horrible school system. They recommend:

1. Vocalize your opinions to all local, state or federal representatives and institutions to minimize the ruthless influence of unions and leftwing politicians in our school.
2. Support our conservative worldview that parents are supposed to be the ultimate decision makers in children's education.
3. Confront school or college administrations and don't blindly accept their education plan based on their reputation or glossy marketing.
4. Report teachers or administrators to the school board other authorities if they create an intimidating atmosphere, banning conservative views and push one-sided Marxist ideology on our children.
5. Demand from local schools to accept "The Student Bill of Rights" and "Academic Bill of Rights" as developed by the Students for Academic Freedom.
6. Start your own counter-cultural mission by teaching or assisting in a public school or college.
7. Volunteer by joining the school board, PTA or other educational organizations
8. Try to install a Bible curriculum at your school district. It is still legal and is available through the National Council on Bible Curriculum in Public Schools. Over 1,300 school boards in 39 states have already adopted it.
9. Remove your children from a bad public school and try to find a private alternative if everything fails.

How can we improve our educational system

Our primary focus must be to combat the Marxist worldview oriented curricula and the socialist-style brainwashing of our kids. However, our educational system also displays a series of major systemic problems we should engage. What must be urgently improved?

1. Parents need to be dramatically more involved in all educational matters.
2. Standard core curriculum (adopted in 19th century) must be updated to fit current educational needs and to be efficiently organized. Only well-organized curriculum leads to a productive learning experience.
3. Standard core curriculum should also challenge moral and ethical questions we face today.
4. The use of technology must be more standardized, up-to-date and practical.
5. School spending should follow more actual needs and common educational sense.
6. Teacher training must be adapted to the 21st century.
7. Education must be much more innovation-oriented.
8. Educational institutions must start thinking outside of the box.
9. We must find solutions how to handle school dropouts.
10. We must evaluate if and how teacher tenure is benefitting students.
11. Educators should re-evaluate the idea of year-round-schooling.
12. We must find way to avoid the terrible overcrowding of some schools.

How to restore free speech at our colleges

Freedom of speech is a fundamental American freedom and a human right, and there's no place where this right should be more valued and protected than in America's colleges and universities, the Foundation for Individual Rights in Education (FIRE) states.

"A university exists to educate students and advance the frontiers of human knowledge, and does so by acting as a "marketplace of ideas" where ideas compete. The intellectual vitality of a university depends on this competition—something that cannot happen properly when students or faculty members fear punishment for expressing views that might be unpopular with the public at large or disfavored by university administrators."

Free speech, freedom of expression and freedom of thought are under continuous threat at most universities and colleges. Why?

Most people can't understand why our colleges and universities fight the free speech and democratic exchange of intellectual ideas. It does not make any sense, it's totally illogical – unless you discover the reason.

And the reason is crystal clear. In the sixties, the Marxist worldview at the academia was in minority. Therefore, they needed free speech in order to promote their socialist mindset. That's why one of the worst colleges by today's standards, Berkeley, used to be the birthplace of "free speech and freedom" movement.

Nowadays, ninety percent of our academic administrators, faculty members and students are socialists. They don't need free speech in order to make their points anymore. They are in charge, and free speech would only benefit their conservative opposition. For them, free speech is counter-productive to Marxism.

This is a method we can watch in all totalitarian societies. They use free speech and democracy as long as they benefit from it. As soon as they are in power, they dismiss it as not necessary anymore.

Turkish president Erdogan described this fascist attitude perfectly when he admitted publicly that "democracy is like a subway. Very useful until you reach the point where you want to be. Then, you exit..."

Campus Reform does an excellent job in promoting traditional constitutional values on US campuses. They need much more support from politicians as well as general public. We all must support them by becoming activists promoting democracy, freedom, free speech and the American Way of Life:

1. First Amendment guaranteeing free speech, freedom of the press, peaceful assembly and the right to petition.
2. Freedom of religion, enabling you to follow any religion of your choice. The religious liberty is a cornerstone of the US society.
3. Freedom of conscience by providing the right to think and believe any way you want - without being forced to conform to any governmental or societal group thinking opinions.
4. Due process in order to guarantee a fair, unbiased and equitable procedure in determining somebody's guilt or innocence. Due process must be applied in all college judicial proceedings.

The problem is perfectly described in the book "The Shadow University: The Betrayal of Liberty on America's

Campuses" by Alan Charles Kors and Harvey A. Silverglate.

How to oppose Marxist Feminism

Feminism started as a good thing for the entire society. Voting rights for women, equal treatment under the law, respect and equal opportunity in all areas of our life – who would honestly oppose to that?

Feminism brought, not unlike unions, a series of valuable accomplishments to our humanity. This was decades ago when feminism was what it is supposed to be: a genuine activism for women's rights, but not a radical, men-hating, political leftwing fringe group focusing on Marxist ideals only.

Feminists claim there is sexism in America. For years, feminists are promoting the "equal pay" myth, claiming that women are paid averagely 19% less than men. This is based on a 2010 Bureau of Labor Statistics data, but they conveniently miss that this is an average of all men's and women's jobs. This compares apples to oranges. Why?

They conveniently don't consider that millions of women purposely chose jobs with less hours, less responsibility and, of course, less pay. The reason is self-evident: they are mothers who don't sacrifice their family duty for their career and therefore don't make as much. These statistics are deceitful and worthless.

In reality, there are many other factors that affect pay. Generally, men and women tend to gravitate toward different industries. Women often work in lower-paying sectors of the economy. New statistics show that men generally work longer hours than women. This is part of the explanation, too.

Fact: If you compare identical jobs in identical industries, women nowadays earn the same pay as men.

Decades ago, feminist proponents insisted women should have same rights and opportunities as men. Virtually nobody objected to that seriously. Nowadays, organizations like NOW (National Organization for Women) push the talking point that all women are "victims."

Interestingly, this perfectly coincides with Marxist worldview and the platform of the Democratic Party in the US. The new, radical feminist ideology does not help but hurt women. Why?

The bitter cynicism of the radical feminist agenda tells women that they are supposed be and behave like men. The first logical contradiction starts here. They criticize men, hate men, despise views and actions of men, but still want to become like them. Where is the logic?

Philosophically, the main pillar of feminism is supposed to be women's dignity. The new NOW philosophy does not include any family-oriented role of women as wives, mothers or housekeepers, the traditional and most important aspect of life.

They don't need men, they don't need to have boyfriends, they don't need to get married, and they don't need to have kids. This pretty much sounds like a lesbian agenda.

Instead, they are supposed to behave like men: no commitment, casual sex, and no family aspirations. Contradiction: This is exactly what they hate men for.

How feminists became enemies of the women

This new Marxist ideology of radical feminism will result in the death of feminism. Their men-hating fixation distracts from real issues they may have. Feminist men bashing has become a frequent misogynistic type of platitude not many take seriously anymore.

They criticize men in all aspects of their lives: personal behavior, how they think, how they act, how they talk, how they walk, how they approach relationships and more. This sweeping generalization is filled with hostility. Many men are reacting accordingly. They object to:

1. Cynicism that radical feminists display toward men
2. Criticism of masculinity
3. Demand for "emasculation" of men
4. Neo-masculine appearance of women
5. Gender confusion disregarding biological facts

Many sociologists are worried about the increasing personal detachment between men and women.

More and more, married women are increasingly going out with girlfriends instead of men, and go on vacation with other women instead of husbands.

This trend is not a financial problem but a sociological and psychological one. Women go overboard. Men give up. Is this our future?

How biological facts don't matter anymore

Any public discussion of gender topics is highly fashionable among the progressive left. This has almost nothing to do with the natural assignment of the sex at the birth of a child. A radical "social change" agenda promoted by the Marxist-oriented left, progressives, gay, lesbians, transgenders and the media dominate the talking points. Let's clarify the terms first:

1. Sex is a biological status determined by the birth: male or female
2. Gender is a socially constructed term describing societal role and behavior
3. Transgender is an "umbrella" for people who don't conform to the birth assigned sex and mostly demand medical "sex change" such as hormone therapy and sex change surgery
4. Gender identity is mind-based feeling, an internal urge to associate with a specific sex such as male, female or "something else"

In accordance with lesbian and transgender policies, radical feminists are approaching their problem from three competing and contradicting sides:

1. Hatred of masculinity
2. Promotion of the female version of "masculinity"
3. Rejection of the natural male-female gender distinction

For Marxists and feminists, gender is not a biological fact but a "social construction society used to oppress women". Feminists claim that the society "assigns" gender through language, clothing, toys and gender-specific roles they are supposed to play.

"Gender is a socially constructed phenomenon", lesbians, trans-genders and feminists claim. For them, just the description "women" is oppressive. Many of them demand a total elimination of women gender. Their problem: male privilege and sex distinction.

Disregarding the law of logic, feminists are stuck between two competing desires of being either "women" or "genderless" human beings; without determining the factor of appropriate genitalia for each gender.

How is the left destroying our families

The most radical feminists nowadays do not act much from the prospective of biology, tradition or common sense. They perform much more as Marxist-oriented provocateurs that have more sympathy for utopist-type of "social change" than for every day's reality.

When some of their most vocal protagonists state that "having children is the worst thing women can do to the planet", everybody acknowledges that they are totally detached of reality.

Feminists don't care about a series of measures really hurting women:

1. Feminists heartlessly support abortions
2. Feminists don't care about unborn human life
3. Feminists are numbed about the Muslim FGM (female genital mutilation)
4. Feminist don't oppose the ruthless Islamic oppression of women through Sharia law

Our reaction is not a surprise. Thousands of women have left the movement, most conservative people wrote them off, and their membership has shrunk to a minimum of leftwing radicals.

Also, highly discouraging is men's withdrawal. They became uncomfortable with their own girlfriends or spouses and chose to withdraw socially themselves from a typically common partnership life.

They flee into video games, pornography, reality television, spectatorships or sports. They can't take the cynicism anymore and morph into pseudo-psychopaths and depression. It's easy to see the negative consequences this kind of behavior has on our children.

Our feminist agenda is missing one crucial point: men and women need each other, not just for sex and human reproduction. They are supposed to be equal partners in life. As Tammy Bruce, resigned board member of NOW, once said, "Women civilize men..."

How to restore our freedoms

How to find out what is killing America

As described extensively in my latest book "Find Peace of Mind or Lose Your Mind – How to survive the collapse of our values, morals and principles" (available as paperback or e-book), most Americans feel that all major aspects of our American Way of Life have gone down the drain. Not much is as it used to be few decades ago. Everything is changing for the worse. This did not happen by accident. Major political forces are at play.

How to uncover it's not about left vs. right

The main problem in our political discussion worldwide is the highly deceptive distinction of "left versus right." It is catastrophically misleading like the description "liberal" which is nowadays almost the opposite of unbiased. Leftist today belong to the most close-minded, intolerable fascist-like people in politics if you consider how they treat their opposition. Nowadays, "liberals" are not liberal at all.

About left and right: They extreme left (communists) and extreme right (fascists) are not opposites. They are both dictatorships. Socialists and "national socialists" (Nazis) are equally socialists. They are both anti-freedom. This is what we all should argue.

1. The correct description of our political struggle is the fight between personal freedom and totalitarianism.
2. Let's stop talking about left and right. Let's start discussing our fight between personal freedom movements and totalitarian state-controlled government like socialism or fascism.

How to expose ego-trips on steroids

The crucial problem is that everybody has his own agenda. This does not preclude that every agenda is "bad", but most of them actually are. If you try to analyze our public brainwashing that we face 24/7 in virtually all aspects of our life, two main culprits show up: "cultural Marxism" and "cultural relativism" accompanied with "political correctness."

This shows four major conflicts with our Constitution we urgently must start attacking:

1. Genophilia: Absolute preference for any non-white race
2. Cultural identity: Ethnicity-based pseudo-religious worldview
3. Leukophobia: Irrational fear of whites
4. "Blood-related" nation definition: Refusal of a "melting-pot" national structure like USA

Marxism-oriented radical agitation groups such as "Media Matters", "Center for Media and Democracy", Antifa or Southern Poverty Law Center have very successfully influenced our public discourse by planting their agenda-driven talking points and arguments in politics and social life. They receive millions of dollars in support by the Hungarian communist entrepreneur George Soros and several Marxist non-profit organizations.

How the left is attacking wrong problems and demanding dishonest solutions

Our public discussion is primarily dominated by totally wrong problems. Even much worse, with completely unsuitable solutions. We must fight back!

1. For our media and the entire leftwing movement, "Islamophobia" (unreasonable fear of Islam) is a major problem in the US and not the Islamization of the Western culture and Christianity. This is despite the fact that Muslims cause a major political, social and other problems, including deadly terrorism in all countries worldwide where they are a minority.

2. Their "solution" therefore is to kill any doubts or criticism of Muslim culture in our society, but not the permanent attempt of the Islamic takeover of our society by Islamic Sharia law. Like in Canada and some European countries, criticism of Islam will be criminalized.

One of the perfect arguments: As Prager University brilliantly describes, anarchists, communists, socialists and other fascist movements never attack the real problem such as poverty and crime in democratically dominated areas like Detroit or Chicago. They constantly complain about "our gun problem," but never acknowledge that guns don't kill people, thugs do.

All democratically lead metropolitan areas are over-saturated with thugs who do not care whether guns are "legal" in "gun-free zones" or not. Laws don't prevent criminals from buying a gun. The black market is full of them. If gun laws worked, why are Houston and Dallas with hundreds of gun store ten times safer than Detroit or Chicago where guns are outlawed?

What did Hitler, Stalin, and Mao do first when they came into power? Like all dictators, they outlawed guns first because tyrants can't afford to allow any kind armed resistance. What does this tell you? It is not about gun control. It's about people control! That's why our founders established the 2nd Amendment in our Constitution.

At the same time, the American feminist movement accuses conservative, traditional Americans of "women hatred," misogyny and gender-related disadvantage in job and business-related matters. They consider themselves as "victims" of our society based on the Constitution and American Way of Life. On the other side, they never attack the real problems of women: Sharia law and the unbearably inhuman mistreatment of women (such as female genital mutilation) in Muslim in other countries.

How is cultural relativism ruining everything

In opposition to the Western culture's philosophy that moral truth is objective and universal, cultural relativism wrongly claims "every culture has its own specific but equally valid mode of perception, thought and choice." There are no "absolutes" and no "right or wrong."

The moral codes depend only on the worldview of each culture or society. Consequently, cultural relativism does not accept "objective standards." No one is entitled to them. Therefore, Judeo-Christian values are not "better or worse" than others such as Islamic values as described in the Sharia Law.

There is no "superior" culture, just "different". According to this worldview, we cannot criticize Hitler, Stalin, China's Tiananmen Square massacre, S. Africa's apartheid, slavery or Islamic genital mutilation. "We cannot judge other cultures by our own worldview," relativists argue.

Karl Marx followed Kant's theory that "each multicultural subgroup has its own reality, own logic, own truth." There is no way to reason among different groups because there is "no universal truth," just each group's own "reality".

This is exactly what America's left practices every day in all shapes and forms.

How is multiculturalism just combating "whiteness"

Multiculturalism is a politicized form of cultural and moral relativism. In reality, it is a dirty trick to fight whiteness and any white majority still in power.
For progressives, all cultures and ethnic backgrounds are "equal", independent of our worldview and value assessment. Claim: Islam is equal to Christianity. There are no moral and ethical differences. Some of the major beliefs of the "Enlightenment" era such as objectivity, reason and evidence are not acceptable anymore.

Multiculturalists in Europe and America categorically dismiss the importance of the Judeo-Christian values and Western civilization as a whole. They accuse it of "elitism and racism" and promote the following political agenda we must counter:

1. Race, ethnicity and sex (or sexual orientation) are inescapable factors of how people think and act. Rational dialogue is impossible because every group has its own "truth."

2. Each ethnic group's "truths" are transcendent, fixed and not changeable. Every group has its own right to establish their own "truth claims."

3. Ethnic origin has its irrevocable attributes and must comply with anti-individualistic group thinking. These theses are non-debatable.

4. Multiculturalism is replacing all individual rights with Marxist-style collectivism.

5. Victimhood presents "cause and effect" of multiculturalism. Victims of Western culture have a perpetual claim on our society and our government.

6. Educational projects and proposals generally view most non-Western cultures as "victims." US Colleges teach non-whites to view themselves as victims of white and capitalist oppression. The common culture or intellectual and moral legacy as found in the Greek and Bible tradition is totally dismissed.

7. Multi-culturists claim "Western oppression" is the problem, there is "nothing positive" about the Western civilization and no American may ever pass any judgment about other cultures.

8. For people believing in multiculturalism, it is absolutely unacceptable to believe that some cultures are "better than others" because reason is better than force, free society is better than slavery or free-market productivity is better than Marxist stagnation.

9. Western academic standards are of no use because they "oppress minorities". Our objective college tests are deemed "racist".

10. High school or college students are taught that there are no objective merits or failings of theories, arguments, policies, literature, art etc. Imperialism, oppression, inequality and revolutionary change" are the key words of Marxist propaganda in the West.

How to stand-up against the reverse racism

For socialists, racial and ethnic identity is the main and often only factor identifying one's identity. All meanings, actions and decisions are supposed to be derived from a person's racial background. This is the main ingredient of "racial diversity," not realizing that "racism" cannot be fought with more racism.

Identity politics promote racial and ethnic division people who are rather supposed to be unified. Martin Luther King's civil rights philosophy to "judge a person by the content of his character and not by the color of his skin" is not valid for America's Marxists anymore.

Trying to discredit the argument that only individualism can be an alternative to racism, the recent claims of "compensation for slavery" by whites totally ignore the fact that virtually all whites are against slavery and that each person is a sovereign entity with their own independent judgment and choice.

The "collective responsibility" of whites for racist actions of their ancestors in the old South many decades ago is a central point of the new agenda. Therefore, all whites must accept a "collective guilt" and are to blame for the slavery Muslim pirates brought to America centuries ago.

How to stop dividing America

Who are we? For over two hundred years, we all considered to be "Americans". Unified, under one flag, one Constitution, one state of mind.

Contrary to most other countries, America used to be the perfect "melting pot" of different races, ethnicities and classes. America survived slavery, civil war, both world wars, Jim Crow and the sixties. Despite major differences, the process unified US citizens rather than dividing individuals.

The wide-spread identity politics brutally promoted by the socialist left constitute a series of aspects we must address. As the Hoover Institution points out, our position in the world is absolutely unique:

1. The Declaration of Independence and the American Constitution are unique documents for their time and proved transcendent across time and space. Both documents preserved the ideal that all people were created equal and were human first, with inalienable rights from God that were protected by government.

2. Our two-ocean-buffer made Americas ability to monitor the numbers of new arrivals and the melting pot's ability to assimilate, integrate, and intermarry immigrants, who would soon relegate their racial, religious, and ethnic affinities to secondary importance.

3. The US is the most individualistic and capitalistic of the Western democracies, blessed with a robust economic growth, rich natural resources, and plenty of space. We assumed that our limited government and ethos of entrepreneurialism would create enough widespread prosperity and upward mobility that affluence would create a common bond superseding superficial Old-World ties based on appearance or creed.

In the sixties, America's left start departing from these principles. As the Hoover Institution states, "This shift from the ideal of the melting pot to the triumph of salad-bowl separatism occurred, in part, because the Democratic Party found electoral resonance in big government's generous entitlements and social programs tailored to particular groups. By then, immigration into the United

States had radically shifted and become less diverse. Rather, than including states in Europe and the former British Commonwealth, most immigrants were poorer and almost exclusively hailed from the nations of Latin America, Asia, and Africa, resulting in poorer immigrants who, upon arrival, needed more government help."

A half century later, this change, combined with affirmative action, lead to a huge identity politics and diversity industry instigating millions in government, academia and private sector to depart from American values and start teaching values of other cultures and other countries.

For the major media and the entire Marxist-oriented left, this was the birth of the mushrooming identity politics. They stopped identifying with the American Way of Life and instead started appealing to different ethnic and social groups Democrats saw as their future voter potential:

1. Blacks
2. Latinos
3. Muslims
4. Gays
5. Lesbians
6. Transgenders

This was the end of the American melting pot mindset. If you don't agree with their identity politics agenda, you were called:

1. Racist
2. Sexist
3. Homophobic
4. Xenophobic
5. Islamophobic

In short, as Hillary Clinton hatefully summarized, a "basket of deplorables". This agenda faces the following facts:

1. Racial solidarity of "non-whites"
2. Expectations that non-whites share the same attitude. The truth is that Cubans don't get along very well with Mexicans, blacks don't agree with the open-border policies and many social aspects.
3. The expected ethnic solidarity could cut in both ways.
4. It is uncertain how the immigration flow will develop in the near future.
5. Factors such as privilege and class are re-emerging.
6. The ideology is eroding the identity politics. One of the reasons is that conservative minority women are not considered "genuine" is because the Marxist ideology supersedes even the leftwing identity politics. Primarily, it's not about protecting the minority identity. It's only to advance the Marxist ideology.

How to fight the dirty stunt: Political correctness

One of the most disturbing parts of social changes in America is left's political "correctness" which objectively means the opposite of "correct". We all just accepted the description naively not suspecting the reason and long-term political effect. Why do we still do that?

In order to reach the Marxist objective, the proponents had to change our logical, objective and traditional descriptions to "politically correct" (Marxist-style) language. This is broadly brainwashing not just our children but also the entire society.

Political correctness is the word of the year. It automatically assumes that all Constitution-based, conservative, traditional family values are "politically incorrect" and therefore must be unequivocally transformed into a politically correct narrative. This description is always based on their Marxist worldview. What does the PC police specifically want?

1. Elitism: They pretend to be morally superior to conservatives
2. Futurism: They pretend to predict the future better than our experienced-based judgment
3. Collectivism: Individuals don't matter, the socialist-style collective must be preferred for a "better good" of the society
4. People control: Their Marxist worldview measures are supposed to control everything from your birth until your death

The main anti-American and anti-democratic political correctness demands are:

1. Do not favor any ethnic group over another
2. Do not infringe on any groups sovereignty
3. Do not interfere with any minority group
4. Do not hinder society to protect specific cultural groups
5. Do not promote any ethnic or cultural "stereotypes"

How is victimhood used as a weapon against us

All victims are told that their personal failures are not the result of their insufficient effort or hard work but only the product of unfair conditions by our racism, unfairness and white-dominance. Some colleges teach students that human accomplishments are no longer as important as the politically correct thinking in life.

Political correctness affects the foundation of American society in a highly negative way. Altering our vocabularies, affirmative action, multicultural education and other measures hurt our academic structure and education at large.

Such actions perfectly explain the "logic" of the "Black life matters" movement. "All life matters" is racist, Marxist progressives propagate. Their indirect logical conclusion is that "white life" does not matter. This is what their radical racist thinking indicates, even though they rarely openly admit this. Their logic is upside down.

How is social engineering destroying America

The idea of deconstructionism is the effort of dismantling and devaluing our system of human and academic integrity. After the "objectivity" has been discredited as "myth," everything depends on "societal values." Their literature became a tool of promoting for Marxist ideological ideas.

Postmodernism denies the ability to know anything but yourself. Therefore, it declares "universal tolerance of all ideas" (except traditional ones). Some proponents believe that there is only a "socially constructed reality". There are no "universal truths," they say.

All our current civil rights demands reflect social engineering perfectly. It is exclusively grounded on Marxist philosophy:

1. Collectivism
2. Identity politics
3. Determinism (no personal responsibility for actions)
4. Economic egalitarianism

5. Elitism
6. Victimization

As irrational social engineering is, it claims to affect our intellect, morality and dedication for the "common good" (like all socialist ideas do). This philosophy is highly illogical and extremely dangerous for our society. Catastrophic consequences must be expected. Therefore, we must fight them.

How to reclaim our civilization

Ignoring the fact that the traditional marriage is and was the fundamental cornerstone of virtually all cultures for millennia, the attacks on our way of life have been relentless.

Our Marxism-based secular society views marriage as the predominately Christian tradition "incompatible with modern lifestyle". Why? People with no family ties are mostly unhappy and therefore much easier to manipulate! In Marxism, everything is about power and manipulation of the collective.

For secularists in politics, media and other portion of our society, marriage is just an "option" for Christians, patriots, traditionalists and right wingers. Like in most aspects of our culture war, we are losing the info war. We can partially blame ourselves for not defending what is sacret to us sufficiently enough.

The history of our family structure is based in the Christian tradition and the Bible. Unfortunately, arguing with religious arguments causes most opposition by Marxism-admiring left wingers.

How are families always better off?

Studies have shown countless benefits of a married life:

1. More happiness for all
2. Longer life
3. Better mental health
4. Less heart attacks
5. Less strokes
6. Lower stress levels
7. Children will love you more
8. Better surgery recovery

9. Better sleep
10. Better sex
11. Greater safety for all
12. Financial stability

There are many financial factors making a traditional family structure much better than a single's life. Let's view this from a pure financial aspect:

1. Child tax credit
2. Child and dependent care tax credit
3. Offsetting childcare cost by using flexible spending accounts
4. Social security benefits for married people
5. Extra tax deductions
6. Less estate taxes
7. No gift tax for your spouse
8. Inheritance benefits
9. More advantageous IRA contribution opportunities
10. Double capital gain tax deduction for married couples

Stable families also mostly produce financial stability, which on the other side leads to major advantages for all family members.

1. Positive energy
2. Less stress and better health
3. Better marriage life
4. More options for all
5. More generosity
6. More stable children's personalities

How to defend our family structure

Sociologists teach us that there are basically four ways to approach your defense of the marriage and traditional family life. All of them are very powerful, but they produce different results at diverse worldviews of your discussion partners.

1. Biblical evidences
2. Physical facts
3. Sociological perspectives
4. Economic arguments

Start everything by asking yourself this important general question: Why is defending the traditional family structure so crucial for the future of our nation?

1. All societies in the history of mankind rejecting the family structure have failed terribly and suffered grave consequences.
2. Marriage and family provide essential benefits to all.
3. Marriage is not a denial of individual rights to others but a source for a common good.
4. A strong family life offers vital benefits for the economic survival, mental and emotional health of all family members.
5. The family structure is an existential part of our civilization.

It is extremely important that you build your own strategy and tactics how to proceed.

1. Strategy is your actual campaign plan you intend to use.
2. Tactics are the concrete approach techniques specifying your approach.

Your success will always depend on your approach how do you argue and the way you proceed. As emotional as this topic is, try always to be as objective as you can. Remember: You have the best arguments on the planet. You just have to present them efficiently!

3. Be factual and precise
4. Be respectful to others
5. Let other people talk and listen to them
6. Use a clear and confident voice
7. Use best arguments suitable for the person or group you are talking to.
8. Always be prepared for your confrontation.
9. Research your arguments and counter-arguments carefully ahead of time.

Most conservative activist groups and pro-family organizations have extensive information about the values of a traditional marriage available on their websites. It is absolutely necessary to use these resources.

Among the most persuasive arguments for the importance of marriage are findings of scientific groups or organizations such as the American College of Pediatricians. Their expertise on the physical, mental and social development of children can't be overstated.

1. Children raised in traditional family structure do dramatically better than kids in so-called non-traditional settings.
2. Children need both mother and father for their physical, mental and social well-being.
3. Children are often badly hurt when divorce courts too much depend on the current social science, political arguments and trendy group opinions.

Very helpful are organizations such as Texas Values, defending the traditional marriage, family and parental rights. The following list shows what is important to promote and defend. Information is everything.

1. Christian worldview based marriage information and education before and during marriage.
2. Highlighting the destructive impact of divorce on children with development of policy proposal how to find appropriate solutions.
3. Improving public policy solutions promoting respect and fairness to families including family-friendly tax policy.
4. Protection of unborn life
5. Promoting of raising children in a traditional family setting.
6. Stimulating adoption as the best alternative to abortion.
7. Advocating parental rights in all areas of children's life including education and medical decisions.
8. Guarding religious freedom and US heritage in all stages of education,

How to distribute the Parents' Bill of Rights

The advocacy group TrueTolerance.org has published Parents' Bill of Rights protecting your child from political brainwashing and abuse in Marxist-oriented public schools.

1. Request and arrange time to examine textbooks, lesson plans, curriculum and supplemental materials used in their child's classroom.
2. Request a time to visit the school and observe their child's classes.
3. Meet with teachers, as well as consult with other professionals interacting with their children at

school, including counselors, coaches, administrators, etc.

4. Inspect their child's school records, including academic, counseling and health information.
5. Be notified when medical services are being offered to their child.
6. Be notified if the school is aware that their child has been bullied or has been accused of bullying.
7. Be notified if a criminal action is deemed to have been committed against their child.
8. Be notified if their child is accused of a criminal action or an infraction that warrants a significant form of school punishment, such as detention.
9. Expect and request an educational environment that is emotionally and physically safe for their children.
10. Expect and request an educational environment that respects your child's religious freedoms.
11. Be informed of and have the right to appeal school policies and administrative decisions.
12. Receive written notice and the option to opt their child out of surveys that include invasive questions about students' sexual experiences or attractions, their families' beliefs, morality, religion, political affiliations or mental and psychological problems of the student or family members.
13. Request a change in class or teacher assignment for their child.
14. File a request for information from the school under the Freedom of Information Act
15. Be notified if their child is absent from school or classes.
16. Have the opportunity to volunteer or participate on review committees that made decisions about curriculum, lesson plans and books.
17. Receive written notice and have the option to opt their child out of controversial instruction on

topics such as sex education, sexual orientation and homosexuality-related instruction.
18. Know, which extracurricular clubs and school activities their children are participating in

How to use the Academic Bill of Rights

David Horowitz Freedom Center developed the Academic Bill of Rights Marxists ferociously object to. The reason is because it limits their now virtually unopposed domination of their political activism in our colleges and universities.

1. All faculty shall be hired, fired, promoted and granted tenure on the basis of their competence and appropriate knowledge in the field of their expertise and, in the humanities, the social sciences, and the arts, with a view toward fostering a plurality of methodologies and perspectives. No faculty shall be hired or fired or denied promotion or tenure on the basis of his or her political or religious beliefs.

2. No faculty member will be excluded from tenure, search and hiring committees on the basis of their political or religious beliefs.

3. Students will be graded solely on the basis of their reasoned answers and appropriate knowledge of the subjects and disciplines they study, not on the basis of their political or religious beliefs.

4. Curricula and reading lists in the humanities and social sciences should reflect the uncertainty and unsettled character of all human knowledge in these areas by providing students with dissenting sources and viewpoints where appropriate. While teachers are and should be free to pursue their own findings and perspectives in presenting their views, they should consider and make their

students aware of other viewpoints. Academic
disciplines should welcome a diversity of
approaches to unsettled questions.

5. Exposing students to the spectrum of significant
    scholarly viewpoints on the subjects examined in
    their courses is a major responsibility of faculty.
    Faculty will not use their courses for the purpose
    of political, ideological, religious or anti-religious
    indoctrination.

6. Selection of speakers, allocation of funds for
    speaker's programs and other student activities
    will observe the principles of academic freedom
    and promote intellectual pluralism.

7. An environment conducive to the civil exchange
    of ideas being an essential component of a free
    university, the obstruction of invited campus
    speakers, destruction of campus literature or other
    effort to obstruct this exchange will not be
    tolerated.

8. Knowledge advances when individual scholars are
    left free to reach their own conclusions about
    which methods, facts, and theories have been
    validated by research. Academic institutions and
    professional societies formed to advance
    knowledge within an area of research, maintain
    the integrity of the research process, and organize
    the professional lives of related researchers serve
    as indispensable venues within which scholars
    circulate research findings and debate their
    interpretation. To perform these functions
    adequately, academic institutions and professional
    societies should maintain a posture of
    organizational neutrality with respect to the
    substantive disagreements that divide researchers

on questions within, or outside, their fields of inquiry.

Organizations such David Horowitz Freedom Center and TrueTolerance.org offer a wealth of valuable information for freedom and liberty-loving people.

Search for help on how to protect your parental rights. The following progressive advocacy groups flood our schools and colleges with slanted educational material intended in order to promote anti-family viewpoints.

What to watch in our schools

1. Gay and lesbian organizations
2. National Education Association
3. Planned Parenthood
4. SIECUS (Sexuality information and education council of the US)

Legally, their information may brainwash your kids and also put schools in danger of violating constitutional principles and parental rights. The reasons could be because they:

1. Present negative portrayals of some religions and/or give favorable portrayals of other religious or spiritual beliefs.
2. Promote school activities that would single out or ostracize religious and/or socially conservative students.
3. Politicize the school environment with lobbying campaigns and one-sided. messages on political and controversial issues.
4. Sexualize classes with one-sided messages promoting homosexuality, bisexuality, transgenderism, etc., while excluding other viewpoints.

Excellent information also offers the excellent non-profit ParentalRightsFoundation.org. Also, the Alliance Defending Freedom points out that you have the following parental rights:

1. Choose the school environment that best fits your child's needs, whether public school, charter school, private school, or homeschooling.
2. Depending upon where you live, opt your child out of curriculum that would force them to violate your family's religious beliefs.
3. Depending upon where you live, review the curriculum and teaching materials for any of your child's classes.
4. Opt your child out of any extracurricular activity.
5. Depending upon where you live, be notified if your child is enrolled in a course that includes sex education, family planning, homosexual themes, diversity issues, or extreme violence.
6. Access your child's record, including grades, disciplinary, and counseling proceedings.
7. Remove your child on days of religious observance.
8. Depending upon where you live, receive the same tax credits and vouchers to attend religious schools available to attend non-religious schools.

How is education important in a marriage

A healthy marriage offers countless advantages for the entire family. One of them is that marriages of educated people last much longer than others. According to a study by the National Center for Health Statistics, the gain is clear:

1. 78% of college educated women stay married for at least twenty years.

2. Only 40% of women with High School degree or less can claim the same.

Interestingly, college educated women are more likely to get married. Of course, a traditional family also benefits children dramatically. Within a healthy family structure, they enjoy learning major aspects of family life and human decency:

1. Communicating with family members about any potential problems.
2. Respectfully value other people's opinions and emotions.
3. Trusting other people without the need to "prove" each-others trustworthiness.
4. Honesty in talking to each other.
5. Equality by making common decisions holding each other to the very same standards.
6. Enjoying family time without hurting your own privacy.

There is a dramatic difference between children growing up in traditional family settings versus families and kids in single-parent homes or other non-conventional arrangements. The Institute for American Values undertook an extensive review about the family structure and children's educational outcomes.

Unfortunately, there is a sharp increase of single-parenting homes in the US and abroad. Since the 60s it has almost doubled. The effect is upsetting.

1. Preschool kids from traditional families do better and have much less behavioral problems.
2. Elementary school children from non-traditional settings are weaker and display more problems.

3. High School graduates from classic families show a much better achievement and less teenager-style misbehavior.
4. College students from dysfunctional families do not perform as well. Their college attendance also is much lower.

The reasons for this kind of under-performance of kids growing up in non-traditional families are staggering. They have often major and long-lasting psychological problems such as:

1. Higher stress rate
2. Anxiety
3. Depression
4. Low self-esteem
5. Higher probability of illegal activities
6. Higher sexual activity
7. Higher teen pregnancy rate

The Institute summarizes the problem as follows: "Family structure clearly influences educational outcomes for U.S. children. The weakening of U.S. family structure in recent decades, driven primarily by high and rising rates of unwed childbearing and divorce, has almost certainly weakened the educational prospects and achievements of U.S. children. Put more positively, there is a solid research basis for the proposition that strengthening U.S. family structure in the future – increasing the proportion of children growing up with their own, two married parents – would significantly improve the educational achievements of U.S. children."

How is abortion killing human life

Abortion is one of the most discussed hot topics of our generation. The political polarization in our society has reached a point where a rational discussion is barely possible, but actually only a rational and factual discussion can lead to a solution. There are many reasons why abortion is wrong. But where do you get the appropriate information? If you google the topic, you see mostly factually slanted, pro-abortion political disinformation.

Let's get some facts straight, provided by the Guttmacher Institute:

1. 1.1 million abortions are performed in the US annually.
2. Almost one in four pregnancies end in an abortion.
3. About 50% of women seeking an abortion already had one in the past.
4. US has some of the highest abortion rates
5. 51% if abortions are done on women less than 25 years of age.
6. About one of three women had an abortion by the age of 45.
7. Abortion affects black and Hispanic women disproportionally.

The abortion methods are extremely cruel and inhuman. Nevertheless, the political left is considering them a "women's health choice" and a "normal medical procedure". Here are the methods used to kill the baby in the womb:

1. Dilation abortion
2. Partial birth abortion
3. Hysterotomy abortion
4. Intracardial injection
5. Prostaglandin abortion
6. RU-486 abortion
7. Saline injection abortion
8. Suction abortion

All of them are unbelievably brutal and incompatible with ethics and human decency. All of them pose a series of medical risks such as:

1. Heavy bleeding
2. Infection
3. Incomplete abortion
4. Damage to the cervix
5. Scarring of the uterine lining
6. Uterine perforation
7. Damage to internal organs
8. Pelvic inflammatory disease
9. Endometritis
10. Even death

Some studies suggest that you may face additional medical problems down the road:

1. Breast cancer
2. Cervical, ovarian or liver cancer
3. Placenta problems
4. Ectopic pregnancy

These problems may occur in addition to a series of emotional problems:

1. Eating disorders
2. Relationship problems
3. Guilt
4. Depression
5. Flashbacks
6. Suicidal thoughts
7. Sexual dysfunction
8. Alcohol or drug abuse

The Pennsylvania Pro Life Federation emphasizes on the following facts about the abortion:

1. The US Constitution guarantees "right to life" for all, including the preborn babies.
2. Science proves that life begins at conception all nine months of pregnancy
3. Most Americans oppose this limitless abortion law.
4. About one million abortions are performed each year in the US.
5. Abortion is very traumatic to the physical, emotional and spiritual health of women.

For virtually every conscious Christian, abortion is plain murder.

1. All humans are equal and deserve equal protection
2. Abortion is absolutely incompatible with God's word
3. Abortion is child's sacrifice
4. Sciences proves that abortion is killing a human being

Some of the most popular Christian arguments against the abortion are:

1. Life does not belong to us, it belongs to God
2. Human life is special because humans are created in the image of God
3. The Bible affirms "life" in the womb
4. Latest science affirms life beginning at conception

Even the secular morals and ethics object to abortion procedures:

1. Fetus is a human being
2. There is no objective distinction between "person" and "human being"
3. All humans possess human rights

4. The position of the baby in mother's body or outside does not matter morally, ethically and legally

How to promote adoption as alternative to abortion

Countless girls get suddenly pregnant when they are too young, too poor or too busy. They might be still at school, struggling to get their college degree – or have otherwise no means to support a child. The situation seems hopeless. But there is Planned Parenthood. They would be happy to abort their pregnancy! Are they really a solution?

Desperate girls and women are easy prey for them. There is no doubt, there are situations in life, when a pregnancy and birth of a child can't be realistically managed, but this does not mean you have to kill your baby in order to solve your problem!

The adoption offers a solution and many benefits. The American Pregnancy Association defines the advantages of an abortion – most importantly for the unborn child:

1. Saving child life as opposed to the killing by abortion
2. Love and support through adoptive parents who are financially and emotionally prepared to be parents
3. Family-style home environment
4. Two-parent home potentially including brothers and sisters
5. Physical resources and provisions otherwise financially not possible
6. Greater chance to get a good education

Advantages for birth parents who might consider abortion:

1. Prenatal and delivery expenses covered

2. Superior medical care
3. Legal expenses covered
4. Ability to choose a family in accordance to own personal preferences
5. Access to support groups
6. Access to counseling
7. Potential housing assistance
8. Providing happiness to others
9. Opportunity to pursue own dreams

Benefits for the adoptive family:

1. Joy and blessing by adding a child to the family.
2. Opportunity to observe all aspects of the pregnancy otherwise not possible.
3. Chance to experience the gift of raising a child.

How to defend faith in our daily life

In our more and more secular society, it has become less and less popular to openly demonstrate faith - like Laura Ingraham does with her cross on her breast every day. What happened to us? Is going along with the anti-faith trend in the media and social networks more important than "doing the right thing"?

Everything depends on the worldview. Materialism is not compatible with spirituality. It promotes selfishness, egoism and superficiality. Only the Biblical worldview produces the positive energy every family needs.

1. Faith fosters long-lasting marriages
2. Faith offers shared heritage to all family members
3. Faith creates opportunities for family togetherness
4. Faith provides protection and meaning in difficult times
5. Faith leads to a shared social network especially important to kids

How to practice family values every day

Practicing and promoting family values start with your own family rules. Do you have them?

1. Promote positive energy
2. Reward positivity
3. Discourage whining and complaining
4. Teach respect to others
5. Raise the spirits
6. Nix name calling
7. Enforce appreciation
8. Practice transparency
9. Teach honesty
10. Concentrate on self-improvement
11. Encourage the family to improve together
12. Inspire facing discomfort head-on
13. Discourage selfishness
14. Keep each other accountable
15. Demonstrate humility
16. Change habits if necessary
17. Listen first
18. Listen more
19. Seek to understand
20. Explain things politely instead of instructing others vigorously
21. Communicate with clarity
22. Avoid talking too much
23. Teach kids to say more with less words
24. Let kids seek information before making any assumptions
25. Make time to reflect
26. Discuss important family matters
27. Revisit some problems later again
28. Coach and practice patience
29. Live and work smarter – nor harder
30. Experiment and find routines beneficial to all family members

31. Train your family to engage in family activities
32. Learn how to most efficiently expand your physical, mental and emotional capacity
33. Try to create an aesthetically pleasing and peaceful home environment
34. Show gratitude
35. Express gratitude loud and clear when appropriate
36. Do always the right thing
37. Parents choose the best thing for the family in the long-run
38. Apologize with humility when appropriate
39. Correct mistakes when others don' notice
40. Show generosity to others with time, money and kind words

How to each your kids to respect family values

Many children nowadays grow up without real guidance. In broken-down families, nobody teaches them the most important character-building rules such as "right and wrong" anymore. For the communism-inspired radical left, there is no such thing as right or wrong – just "different". We must fight this sick ideology by teaching kids:

1. Honesty
2. Justice
3. Helping others
4. Consideration
5. Sharing
6. Respect
7. Kindness
8. Courage
9. Generosity
10. Responsibility

How to combat media bias against family values

A very hostile bias against everything traditional, conservative or non-progressive dominates our news cycle 24/7. It is often very difficult to find out the actual nature of a story because most of the so-called mainstream media editorializes the news instead of reporting the facts. The difference between the actual news reporting and editorials is barely recognizable. This happens through several forms of bias such as:

1. Purposely ideologically slanted reporting in accordance with personal views of the writer
2. Total omission of specific stories or facts not in agreement with the ideology of the journalist
3. Placement of the story in the media

Most media consumers are clueless how far reaching the political info war already advanced. What can you do? Cancel the newspaper subscription or switch the TV channel. There aren't many options in addition to Fox News Network (FNN) or America One Network (OAN).

If you want to protect our American Way of Life, you must also become an activist.

1. Complain to the highest media brass at TV and radio stations, newspaper or magazines who offend conservative values as intensively and often as you can
2. Cancel a subscription and/or tune them out
3. Write letters to the editor
4. Complain to the top decision makers at companies supporting the bias media with their advertising dollars
5. Engage the bloggers or start an own blog

6. Tape your own interview with the media in order to protect the accuracy of the reporting about you, your cause or company
7. Call conservative talk shows on radio and tell your story

How dangerous are tech giants Google and Facebook?

Virtually all information distributing high tech companies are filled with Marxism-loving youngsters who don't even know what socialism actually does to personal freedoms. In our digital age, most of our information is available only on the web, which is totally dominated by companies such as Google or Facebook. These vast empires don't just make the information searches available. They also manipulate and censor free speech in a dramatically dangerous way. They are our info-war enemies.

1. Determine which information is available online, when and how
2. Manipulate search engine metrics
3. Collect billions of personal data every day
4. Promote Marxist worldview causes
5. Suppress Christian and conservative worldview
6. Disallow transparency
7. Prohibit employees from deviation from their worldview

Example: Google searches about Trump, Republicans, Jews, or Christians are always mostly negative. At the same time, searches about Obama, Democrats, Muslims or atheists are predominantly favorable.

If Facebook sends emails to all leftwing members, this might easily mean 5% of additional votes for Democrats. At the same time, Google can manipulate search results in a way that would affect 10-30% of voters in any election.

How to fight deadly ideologies

The US Constitution and our Bill of Rights are in no way compatible with tyrant-style dictatorships. Therefore, we are the biggest enemy of communism and Islamic fascism. It is natural that they have to fight us in any way possible.

Since they have no chance to win in a fair political competition, they have to fight us in a way communist revolutionaries do. All methods are allowed if they lead to success. Don't expect any kind of peaceful or fair competition!

There is a war out there, a deadly war for influence and brutal power. In many areas of our daily life, we virtually already lost. Our media organizations and education system are widely infiltrated by the Marxist worldview.

How our worldview determines everything

You cannot trust your eyes if your imagination is out of focus (Mark Twain).

Whatever we do or not do, whatever we think, value or hate, how we behave and whatever we believe in or not in our life mainly depends on one thing: our worldview. An oversimplified analogy might be: Whenever we change our eyeglasses, our view of things around us changes because our eyeglasses determine what we are able to see or not to see.

Everybody has a worldview. Rich or poor, smart or stupid, believer or non-believer. All things in our life depend on our worldview. Derived from the German word "Weltanschauung," it refers to a belief system holding all significant concepts of our life such as God, cosmos, knowledge, behavior, values, humanity and history. It is like a kind of a grand perspective of our world and our life.

In more scientific terms, worldview is a mental structure forming our ultimate beliefs. As Resons.org outlines, it provides a general context for life, including a vision of what we consider "authentic" or "real."

Having a normal living requires a well-balanced life, based on realistic assumptions of all basic and critical aspects of our human being. Philosophers identify the worldview as the "big question of life."

According to philosophers, worldview should answer to the following most important questions of our life:

1. Ultimate reality: What kind of God, if any, in fact exists?
2. External reality: Is there anything beyond the cosmos?
3. Knowledge: What can be known – and how can anyone know it?
4. Origin: Where did I come from?
5. Identity: Who am I?
6. Morals: How should I live?
7. Values: What should I consider of greatest worth?
8. Predicament: What is humanity's fundamental problem?
9. Resolution: How can humanity's problems be solved?
10. Past/Present: What is the meaning and direction of history?
11. Destiny: Will I survive the death of my body and if so, in what state?

The answers to such question can provide the focus and purpose of your life as well as logical coherence and reference to reality.

The worldview is much like an optical perspective. The view changes if we switch our position from left to right, from low position to a bird's view. This analogy applies basically to all views and beliefs in our life.

Therefore, we are confronted with countless "perspectives" to virtually all questions of personal and public life. If we are lucky, our media outlets offer us "different viewpoints" to many questions we might be interested in. Some zealots, again and again, want to suggest that these perspectives from their worldview present their "version of truth." The truth, however, does not have any "versions." Truth is truth. Period. Deviation of the truth is just an opinion of a person who wants to bend the actual truth in order to promote own ideology.

Depending on the history, culture, personal background, ideology and religious beliefs, there are many worldviews we encounter every day. There are two basic worldview groups clashing with each other dramatically: religious believers and non-believers. The historically, politically and socially most significant are the Marxist, Muslim, Atheist and Christian worldview.

How to fight back against our enemy #1: Marxism

Lenin himself unmistakably characterizes the Marxist worldview: "Religion is opium for the people. Religion is a sort of spiritual booze…" Communists are atheists, with some exception such as "Liberation theology" in South and Middle America where Christianity is only used as a deceptive tool to reach originally very religious people in this part of the world.

According to Karl Marx, God "does not, cannot and must not exist." In a Marxist worldview, God is considered an "impediment and enemy to a materialistic, socialistic way of life." Following the communist theory, "the humanity is God." "We created God in our own image. We created religion to worship ourselves," Marx states.

As proclaimed in the Communist Manifesto (1848), Marxism totally reflects atheism. As a Marxist, you must be an atheist, propagator of a "God-free" world. Socialists and communists also claim that their materialistic worldview is "scientific".

Generally speaking, the Marxist worldview is virtually identical with the atheist worldview, with the exception of its communist agenda.

An atheist does not to have to be a Marxist, but a communist must be an atheist.

On the basis of this worldview, everything looks different than through the glasses of a Christian society. The Marxist's worldview is based on an unquestionably dominating big government in all parts of life. The state knows better what is good or bad for you. The state makes all-important decisions in your life. The people are "not smart enough" to decide what to learn, what to buy, what to eat, how to behave and what and how to think.

1. Your personal freedoms are meaningless. You must sacrifice them for "the better good" of society. The "collective" is important, and the collective must adhere to all principles of socialism.

2. No free speech, no free press, no free opinion. These are Marxist's ideals, and there is no way around it. In short: Marxist dictatorship is maintained only by brutal force, deception and corruption of human minds.

This worldview, of course, constitutes a major conflict with a free society as declared in our Constitution and our Bill of Rights.

How to learn the best fight back strategy and tactics

We must be courageous, out-of-the-box free-thinkers in order to be able to successfully defeat the cultural Marxism that already dominates most parts of our public life.

Be aware that our efforts are the last resort to save our civilization and our way of life. Do not fear backlash you must expect from the communist-infested public life. Fight back!

1. Feel no shame! Social justice warriors often rely upon shaming tactics to fight conservatives. As long as you don't fear to be called racist, bigot, misogynist, homophobe and more, they can't hurt you much.

2. Don not self-censor! Don't try to be antagonistic in every way, but don't feat to ruffle some feathers on the other side. Let the PC police explode. You should make the point, and if you are logical and factual, you won. By the way, leftists mostly hate facts, logic and common sense because they are mostly weaklings.

3. Make absolutely clear that there is no such thing as white privilege or male privilege! Do not feel guilty just because you might be white or male.

4. Always demand that progressives back up their claims. Virtually without exceptions, Marxists fabricate claims without any proof. We can't allow them to argue publicly with their unverified propaganda. Demand proven facts before you enter the dispute.

5. Don't ever be fooled to play their game. Whenever social justice activists can't follow the logic, they accuse you of "unconscious bias". Example: You as a white and "privileged" person can't ever understand the position of a black man. Therefore, your position is wrong.

6. Don't ever let irrational fears and feelings of Marxists make you "guilty" of something. Why should you give up your rights (such as 2nd Amendment) just because the leftists are "afraid" of guns?

7. Demand unequivocally that our society accepts all of your constitutional rights. Collectivists' propaganda claims that there is no such thing as inherent rights and liberties superseding government rights.

8. Point out that maintaining your rights (such as 1st Amendment), without any doubt, do not hurt other people. PC warriors always claim that your rights have a negative effect on "underprivileged" people.

9. Insist in the fact that any gender assignment is only determined by biological facts and never by socio-political trends of the ultra-left.

10. Don't ever accept the utopian illusion of "equality". People are not a homogenous entity, consisting of individuals who display countless differences.

11. As a man, embrace your natural role of your gender. Don't ever be ashamed of your masculinity and your God-given function in our

society. Resist all feminists' efforts to "feminize" your sons.

12. Always protect individualism vs. socialist-style collectivism. Our society is a collection of individual people who have the right to stay individualists.

13. Avoid group thinking and group behavior under all circumstances. Don't ever act as part of the collective and don't ever fall prey to the claim that social justice warriors fight against the establishment. Marxists always promote a socialist-style government.

14. Home-school your children whenever possible. In most public schools, our kids are brainwashed with the Marxist worldview and might never recover from that.

How to turn the tables

The infamous communist agitator Saul Alinsky created the nasty but in his way brilliant "Rules for Radicals", the widely used manual for communist revolution. Why don't we respond by letting them taste the wrath of their own medicine?

Townhall.com wrote extensively on this topic and how to turn the tables on Saul Alinsky and his followers.

1. Promote a boycott of your enemies! Your actual weapons are not only what you really have but what your opponents' impression is you might use against them. 120 million Americans identify as conservatives and eve n more as Christians. Encourage them to cancel subscriptions, stop watching fake news programs and start boycotting

people and entities who try to destroy the fabric of our country.

2. Don't force your people to go outside of their own experience. Learn from Democrats who use the identity politics at their advantage because their voters understand their message. Create your own Al Sharptons and Jesse Jacksons in order to tap into the minority pool.

3. Force progressives to go outside of their experience. Marxism is an anti-Christian ideology, but 76% of Americans view themselves as Christians! Don't avoid social issues, you can beat Democrats with Christian and family values because they hate them.

4. Beat the Marxists with their own weapons! Don't let the global warming cult leader Al Gore with his mansions and incredible wealth go unopposed.

5. Ridiculing the laughable and fact-less progressive propaganda as what it is: a joke! Make jokes about them. This is one of the most effective weapons in your arsenal.

6. Be extremely creative in choosing your tactics and strategy. In a political discourse, they are often more effective than actual facts. Conservatives usually have all the facts and numbers to make their points, but mostly they are too serious and too boring presenting them.

7. Change tactics and strategy as often as needed. Old approaches often become dull and ineffective.

8. Keep the pressure on your political enemies! Conservatives often make some very effective

arguments, but after the common liberal backlash they mostly easy up on the initiative or give up the points entirely. This is a big mistake.

9. A political threat is sometimes more effective than the real thing. Threaten progressives with consequences of their measures. Tell them how you are going to retaliate or that you intend to sue them. Progressives do that all the time.

10. Don't ever let it go! Keep constant pressure on your opposition. Tell that Bill Clinton is a liar and Barack Obama tried to bankrupt our country again and again. Why do major companies repeat their commercials hundreds of times? Because it's working.

11. The winner is virtually always the party on the offense! Don't ever let you push into defensive. This is viewed as a part of weakness and is rarely rewarded – even if you have the best and most truthful arguments imaginable.

12. Every successful attack must include a constructive alternative. It must be an understandable and workable common-sense idea. Since most conservative programs can be backed up with facts and past experience, this should not pose a problem.

13. Pick the target, freeze, personalize and polarize it – just the way Saul Alinsky taught the revolutionaries. Socialists do this all the time. Why don't we identify Democrats as immoral, anti-family and anti-worker socialists who are at the same time very hostile to Christianity?

How to fight Islamic fascism

The objective of Islamic worldview is to provide the Muslims with the knowledge and explanation of the world as explained in the Koran, to teach people how to achieve main values of Islam, and to establish the fundamental ethical concepts of human existence.

Here are the facts you should use as often and effectively you can in all political, personal, social and "mainstream" media disputes:

1. Everything in the Islamic worldview is based in Allah (Muslims "God"), Mohammed (the prophet) and Koran ("word of Allah").
2. "Islam" means total submission to Allah. No exceptions.
3. Islam is not just a "religion," it is a comprehensive, totalitarian way of life, dictating all aspects of personal, public, political and social life.

From the standpoint of the Western civilization, democracy and human rights, Islam is hardly compatible with Western values, morals and principles. This "clash of civilizations" is grounded in Sharia, the highly controversial Muslim law that, according to Koran, supersedes all other laws, social customs and government regulations all over the world. "There is no other law but Sharia," Islamic scholars strictly declare. Muslims are told that they must adhere to only one law: Sharia.

The Sharia-based Islamic worldview contains a long series of "laws" that we might consider cynical, inhuman or even barbaric. Here is a short list of Sharia strict requirements enforced for every Muslim. Please always point out the following facts:

1. Criticizing or denying Allah is punishable by death
2. Criticizing or denying the Koran or parts of it is punishable by death
3. Criticizing or denying Mohammed is punishable by death
4. A Muslim leaving Islam is punishable by death
5. A Non-Muslim leading a Muslim away from Islam is punishable by death
6. A Non-Muslim marrying a Muslim woman is punishable by death
7. Muslim men can marry and have sex with an infant girl as young as nine years old
8. Female genital mutilation (FGM, cutout of the clitoris) is a must for Muslim girls
9. A Muslim woman can have only one husband, but a man can have up to four wives
10. A Muslim man can divorce his wife anytime, but a wife needs husband's consent to divorce
11. A Muslim wife loses her custody for all children over six-years of age
12. A Muslim man can beat his wife anytime for insubordination
13. If a Muslim woman claims to have been raped, she needs four male witnesses to prove it
14. A raped woman cannot testify in court against the rapist
15. In court proceedings, woman's testimony carries half of the weight of a man
16. Muslim females always inherit just half of what males inherit
17. A Muslim woman is not allowed to drive a car
18. A Muslim woman cannot speak to a man who is not her husband or relative
19. A Muslim woman must prepare every meal containing meat of animals barbarically slaughtered by "Halal"

Muslims are supposed to use the Koran prescribed technique of Taqiyya towards non-Muslims, which encompasses lying and deception if this helps advancing Islam.

Again, the entire Muslim worldview is based on these Islamic principles. This explains drastically, why there are not many "moderate" Muslims around, and why Muslims are not allowed to assimilate into any other culture. As leading Islamic scholars boldly demand, the purpose of Muslim refugees in the West is not to "assimilate," but to "breed" as many children as possible in order to advance Islam worldwide.

This is exactly what happens in all countries accepting Muslim immigration. With virtually no exception, they remain in their own enclaves, maintaining their own culture and practicing Islam as prescribed by Koran.

Even when they live in the US for decades and are naturalized citizens, they practically always identify themselves as "Muslims first." This is the deciding factor for their worldview that our civilization is clashing with.

How to correct our corrupt political system

Corruption is present all-over the world. In most countries, it's much worse, in some somehow better.

What is the definition of corruption? It is illegal, dishonest or fraudulent conduct by people, companies or institutions in power in order to acquire monetary or other benefits at the expense of others. It mostly happens in form of bribery or embezzlement.

How to promote the anti-corruption measures

Corruption is found in all walks of life, but there is no silver bullet for fighting corruption. However, several anti-corruption organizations have developed some useful recommendations. Transparency International advocates the following general anti-corruption measures:

1. End the impunity and allow the law-enforcement to punish people involved in corruption.
2. Reform the public administrations and their financial management in order to more effectively audit government agencies.
3. Promote more transparency of financial dealings.
4. Improve the access to public information
5. Empower citizens by establishing laws demanding anti-corruption measures
6. Close international loopholes in order to avoid money laundering by elected officials, crime organizations and others.

There are many meaningful additional suggestions how to fight corruption in business, private and public life.

1. Ensure appropriate salaries for people in order to discourage the temptation of corruption. This mostly applies to public pay in 3rd world countries where public workers are dramatically underpaid.
2. Immediately dismiss people caught in any kind of corruption.
3. Encourage online e transactions and secure hard copies of everything important.
4. Install security cameras in all sensitive areas where financial transactions can be made.
5. Speed-up work process in business and government institutions.
6. Make the media responsible for practicing their role as an independent watchdog in public life.

Here too, some out-of-the-box ideas might be absolutely necessary to attack the corruption. As "The Guardian" reminds, new technologies might be very helpful in the worldwide struggle against bribery and other forms of corruption.

Deterring corruption with means of technology is a very promising proposition. However, it is not without its own risks, characteristics and potential deceptions.

1. Digitize all applicable public services
2. Automate tax collections and other tasks
3. Share corruption information with all relevant institutions

How to stop the corruption in our political system

The political corruption is so wide-spread all-over the world that you don't know where to start and where to end. Let's limit our examination to the US.

Political lobbyists are villains of the modern politics. Although they are often of the main causes of political corruption, the picture is not cleanly black and white.

Our democratic political system encourages political competition of all candidates. This process, however, requires elaborate political campaigns impossible without major donations.

Of course, political donations are legal and ethical. The problem, however, always arises when political donations exceed the legal and ethical norm. Unfortunately, this is exactly what happens in our political system all the time – from local elections to the highest office in the land.

President Trump started limiting the impact of lobbyists in Washington, but additional strict Congressional measures are over-due. We must urgently review and update our lobbyist system.

1. Lobbyists often raise money for elected officials
2. Lobbyists sometimes even write new laws themselves
3. Lobbyists occasionally bribe politicians with lucrative jobs
4. Lobbyists create a "revolving door" for politicians who take advantage of the financial incentives

Even much worse are "pay-to-play" schemes politicians such as Bill and Hillary Clinton practiced. One of the worst examples in American history is the Clinton deal with the Russian "Uranium One" company, which needed the approval by then Secretary of State Hillary Clinton in order to acquire 20% of US uranium reserve.

In return, Bill Clinton was paid a half million dollars for a short speech in Moscow, and the Clinton Foundation received about 140 million dollars in "donations" by people and companies directly or indirectly involved in Russian uranium business.

American citizens are extremely frustrated by such blatant corruption cases and demand radical reforms of our law. Organizations such as Transparency International have published specific recommendations such as:

1. Transparency of political spending in all areas of financial transactions. This includes real-time information accessible online, political spending by publicly traded companies and financial transactions of political campaigns.
2. Prevention of revolving doors between politicians, lobbyists, and high-level government officials.
3. Disclosure of people and activist organizations behind specific political backers.
4. Establishing a reliable ethics infrastructure through an independent oversight of Government business transactions
5. Legal protection of whistleblowers
6. Maintaining basic public access to Government information

How to prevent voter fraud

Election integrity is essential and the security of the ballot box cannot be left to a simple honor system. It is incumbent upon state governments to safeguard the electoral process, and ensure that every voter's right to cast a ballot is protected, the Heritage Foundation points out.

Contrary to the claims of many liberals, the problem of voter fraud is as old as the country itself. As the U.S. Supreme Court noted when it upheld Indiana's voter identification law, "flagrant examples" of voter fraud "have been documented throughout this Nation's history by respected historians and many journalists." This is a very serious political issue. Only Democrats dispute it, and they have a very good reason. Virtually all fraud cases benefit the left.

1. The right to vote in a free and fair election is the most basic civil right, one on which many other rights of the American people depend.

2. Congress and the states should guarantee that every eligible individual is able to vote and that no one's vote is stolen or diluted.

3. Voter fraud is real and hundreds of convictions have been made and documented.

Political scientists have documented a series of different methods committing voter fraud in the US:

1. Impersonation fraud at the polls
2. Fraudulent registration
3. Duplicate voting
4. Fraudulent use of absentee ballots
5. Buying votes
6. Illegal "assistance" at the voting place
7. Ineligible voting
8. Altering the vote count
9. Ballot petition fraud

Many voting results are so close that a dozen of illegal votes can determine the outcome. This happened many times. Just a few dozens of illegal votes can overthrow the legitimate vote result.

Many illegal aliens from Central and South America are used to socialism in their own homeland. Now, they may want to fulfill their Marxist dream at the expense of American citizens.

Don't you believe that this happens in the US all the time? Just check the heritage Foundation's voter fraud database online. Numerous court convictions for election fraud are documented. Additionally, how come that over 160 of Democratic Counties cast more votes than registered voters?

In the US, state governments are responsible for the election process. We must demand that secretaries of state clean up their voter rolls, which in many Democratic states include thousands of dead people, convicted felons, and illegals.

How to ensure our election integrity

Dozens of non-partisan organizations and thousands of activists already fight for election integrity in the US. The Democratic Party unwaveringly claims that "there I no such thing as election fraud". This mostly applies to virtual "one-party-states" such as California where the "Election Integrity Project California" fights an uphill battle.

They are encouraging legal voters to get involved in eliminating voter fraud. This is what everybody can do to help:

1. Researching state and county voter rolls
2. Educate poll workers and observers about the election law
3. Train poll workers to be more vigilant
4. Send petitions to the legislative committees and other politicians to impact the integrity of the election process
5. Informing the public about the problem, pending measures and voting patters

If you sense any kind of voter fraud or intimidation, you are supposed to report it immediately to:

1. Local FBI office
2. Local US attorney's office
3. The Public Integrity Section of the Dept. of Justice's Criminal Division

The following Federal Voting Rights Laws must be observed:

1. The Civil Rights Acts provide some of the early federal statutory protections against discrimination in voting (42 U.S.C. 1971 & 1974). These protections originated in the Civil Rights Act of 1870 and were later amended by the Civil Rights Acts of 1957, 1960 and 1964.

2. The Voting Rights Act prohibits voting practices and procedures that discriminate based on race, color, or membership in a language minority group. It also requires certain jurisdictions to provide election materials in languages other than English.

3. The voting accessibility for the Elderly and Handicapped Act of 1984 generally requires polling places to be accessible to people with disabilities.

4. Uniformed and Overseas Citizens Absentee Voting Act of 1986 allows members of the U.S. Armed Forces and overseas voters to both register to vote by mail.

5. The National Voter Registration Act of 1993 increases opportunities to register to vote and creates procedures for maintaining voter registration lists, making it easier for people to stay registered.

6. Help America Vote Act of 2002 authorizes federal funds for election administration and creates the Us Election Commission. It also requires states to adopt minimum standards on voting systems, provisional ballots, voter information posters on election days, and for first time voters who register to vote by mail and statewide voter registration databases. The EAC helps states to comply with these requirements.

7. Military and Overseas Voting Empowerment Act of 2009 amends the Uniformed and Overseas Citizens Absentee Voting Act to improve access to voting by military and overseas voters. It requires states to provide electronic access to various parts of the election process, mail absentee ballots to certain voters at least 45 days before an election, and develop a free access system to inform military and overseas voters about whether their voted ballots were received and counted.

All forms of election bribery constitute a criminal offense. Here is the legal description of a state statute describing election bribery:

Any person, who offers, gives, lends or promises to give or lend, or attempts to procure anything of value or any office or employment or any privilege or immunity to, or for, any elector, or to or for any other person, in order to induce any elector to:

1. Refrain from going to the polls.

2. Vote or refrain from voting.

3. Vote or refrain from voting for or against a particular person.

4. Vote or refrain from voting for or against a particular referendum; or on account of any elector having done any of the above.

The solicitation and making of political contributions are heavily regulated under federal law. It shall be a violation of federal law:

1. To knowingly cause or attempt to cause any person to make a contribution of a thing of value (including services) for the benefit of any candidate or party by denying or depriving, or threatening to deny or deprive, that person of any employment, position, or work for any agency or entity of the Federal Government or state or local government, or any compensation or benefit of such employment, position, or work, where such employment, position, or work is made possible in whole or in part by an Act of Congress.

2. To knowingly cause or attempt to cause any person to make a contribution for the benefit of any candidate or party by denying or depriving, or threatening to deny or deprive, that person of any payment or benefit of a federal state, or local program, where such payment or benefit is made possible in whole or in part by an Act of Congress.

3. For certain specified candidates, office holders, officers, and federal employees to knowingly solicit any contribution, as defined by statute, from any other such officer, employee, or person.

4. For certain specified federal officers or employees to make any contribution to any other such officer or employee, or to certain specified federal officeholders if the person receiving such contribution is the employer or employing authority of the person making the contribution.

5. To solicit or receive a contribution for political purposes from any person knowing that that person is entitled to or is receiving compensation,

employment, or other benefits provided for or made possible by an Act of Congress appropriating funds for work relief or relief purposes, or to supply, for political purposes, the names of people receiving such compensation, employment, or other benefits.

6. For an officer or employee of the United States, as defined by statute, to discharge, promote, degrade, or in any manner change the official rank or compensation of any other officer or employee, or to promise or threaten to do so, for giving or withholding or neglecting to make any contribution of money or other valuable thing for any political purpose.

7. To solicit or receive a donation of money or other things of value in connection with a federal, state, or local election from a person who is located in a room or building occupied in the discharge of official duties by an officer or employee of the United States.

As the USLegal.com states, the Federal Election Campaign Act imposes upon the treasurers of political committees the duty to file reports of receipts and disbursements. The Act specifies the contents of such reports. Persons who violate these reporting requirements are subject to criminal penalties under the Act.

How to investigate the union corruption

Every month, millions of union members have taken money out of their paychecks without their approval to support union's political agenda. Virtually all of the funds benefit the Democratic Party – even though a substantial number of union members does not vote left anymore. Political contributions of the unions, especially Public

Employee Unions, go up to a billion each presidential election cycle.

As UnionFacts.com documents, this does not reflect the opinion of American voters or even their own union members:

1. 68 percent of registered voters say they are concerned that public employee unions have too much influence over politicians who, when elected, must negotiate with these groups. (FOX News Poll conducted by Anderson Robbins Research (D) and Shaw & Company Research (R) | March 14-16, 2011)

2. 66 percent of government and private union employees say it is unreasonable that union leaders across America can spend their dues on politics without getting their approval. (The Word Doctors | October 26-28, 2010)

3. 89 percent of private and government union employees agree that union workers should have the right to know how their dues money is being spent and believe the Department of Labor should disclose union spending on the Internet to ensure accountability. (The Word Doctors | October 26-28, 2010)

4. 89 percent of private and government union employees agree that union workers should have the right to know how their dues money is being spent and believe the Department of Labor should disclose union spending on the Internet to ensure accountability. (The Word Doctors | October 26-28, 2010)

5. 69 percent of private and government union employees believe union officials need to stop spending union dues on partisan politics and invest it in creating more jobs, as well as focus on the membership, not the elections. (The Word Doctors | October 26-28, 2010)

It is not widely known that unsatisfied union members can drop their union. This process is called "decertification elections" administered by the National Labor Relations Board (NLRB). The reason for this measure might be because a union is corrupting, undemocratic, violent or just inept.

The United States Dept. of Labor has a hotline to report any kind of unlawful actions by a union such as labor racketeering. Here is the official Inspector General's description:

"The use of a union, benefit plan (i.e. pension plan,) contractor, and/or industry for personal benefit by illegal means. This abuse may take the form of collusive arrangements between union officials and employers that occur at the expense of union members or corruption within the unions themselves. It also occurs when organized crime groups infiltrate unions. "

Forms of union corruption:

1. Criminal abuse of power
2. Extortion
3. Improper collective bargaining agreements.
4. False reports on ERISA required documents.
5. The involvement of a member or associate of a traditional or non-traditional organized crime family or group, or a subject with a felony criminal history in a union.

6. Use of union funds or property for acts of violence.
7. Bribery
8. Payoffs from management to corrupt union officials
9. Coercion of employers by union officials
10. Sweetheart deals
11. Employee Benefit Plan Fraud
12. Embezzlement
13. Kickbacks

How to disclose public unions' "pay-to-play" scheme

Public workers unions represent public employees at every level of our government. Their contract and pensions negotiations are not accomplished under the transparency of the free market. They are able to negotiate directly with politicians who – on the other side – directly depend on union's campaign contributions. A perfect pay-to-play match!

Have you ever asked why public salaries, pensions, and general benefits sometimes exceed the public sector by 50 or more percent? It's obvious.

1. Unions make unreasonably high demands
2. Politician accept union demands
3. Unions, in return, make unreasonably high contributions to the same politicians who made them rich

Over 90% of union's political campaign contributions go directly to Democrats or Democratic causes. This is why this is a shady, immoral and fraudulent alliance, which might be illegal too. OpenSecrets.org documents many specific and highly indicative details about this.

In 2017 alone, public unions spend over 14 million dollars on lobbying on politicians who decide about union contracts. This is the best union "investment" they can make: a corrupt revolving door. Without solving this problem, public budgets will continue to explode, and billions of unfunded liabilities in public pension funds will continue to rise.

Many cities and counties already spend up to 60% of their entire tax income on totally overblown salaries, pensions, and other benefits. There is no end in sight, especially in virtual one-party-states such as California. Democrats are the only ones who could end this train to nowhere, but they benefit from this kind of corruption and won't move a finger to change it.

What can we do? Not much unless we vote the Democrats out of the office. However, in states with a socialist mindset, this remains a pipe dream.

How can we do something against union corruption

As the Detroit Free Press writes, the "UAW, Fiat Chrysler and federal investigators unravel a scandal over the misappropriation of millions of dollars meant for worker training, federal records show that embezzling from union offices is endemic around the country."

According to media reports, U.S. Department of Labor documents obtained by the Free Press show embezzlement from hundreds of union offices nationwide over the past decade. In just the past two years, more than 300 union locations have discovered the theft, often resulting in more than one person charged in each instance, the records show.

Incidentally, two UAW incidents uncovered in 2017, one in Michigan and the other in New Jersey, exceed the $1-

million mark, among the biggest labor theft cases in a decade.

The corruption cases involved unions representing nurses, aerospace engineers, firefighters, teachers, film and TV artists, air traffic controllers, musicians, bus inspectors, bakery workers, roofers, postal workers, machinists, ironworkers, steelworkers, dairy workers, plasterers, train operators, plumbers, stagehands, engineers, electricians, heat insulators, missile range workers and bricklayers.

Statistics show that individual cases compiled by the Office of Labor-Management Standards last year cite theft and fraud ranging from $1,051 to nearly $6.5 million. This is not a pocket change.

Another disturbing example is the case of UFCW Local 700 in Indianapolis. Their board suspected that their president and secretary-treasurer misused funds for their personal benefit. They conducted a secret internal review and found the truth. The Heritage Foundation compiled the findings what they did:

1. Allowed the local's general treasury to shrink to just $100,000 and subsidized the general treasury with unauthorized transfers from the strike fund.

2. Spent hundreds of thousands of dollars from the general treasury without executive board authorization.

3. Made political contributions in excess of legal limits and transferred money from the general treasury to political accounts without authorization.

4. Used money from the local's strike fund to pay for personal meals.

5. Used union funds to pay president's flight, hotel,
    and $1,200 entry fee for a charity golf tournament
    in Montreal.

6. Collected double reimbursement from Local 700
    and the international union for airfare, hotel, and
    meal expenses at the Democratic National
    Convention in Boston.

7. Allowed union contracts to expire without
    bargaining for new ones.

Usually, we can only find out facts about such a corruption
through whistleblowers. We already have well-established
whistleblowers protection laws on the books.

1. Age Discrimination in Employment Act
2. Americans with Disabilities Act
3. Civil Rights Act of 1964 (Title VII)
4. Clayton Act (antitrust)
5. Clean Air Act
6. Comprehensive Environmental Response,
    Compensation and Liability Act ("Super Fund")
7. Employee Retirement Income Security Act
8. Energy Reorganization Act
9. Equal Pay Act
10. Fair Labor Standards Act (Wage and Hour, Child
    Labor, Minimum Wage, Overtime)
11. False Claims Act
12. Family and Medical Leave Act
13. National Labor Relations Act
14. Occupational Safety and Health Act
15. Safe Drinking Water Act
16. Sarbanes–Oxley Act
17. Solid Waste Disposal Act
18. Toxic Substances Control Act

You would think that the current whistleblower protection laws are more than sufficient, but don't hold your breath. As the Heritage Foundation points out, one group of employees is conspicuously absent from whistle-blower protections: employees of labor unions.

Existing whistle-blower provisions prohibit retaliation against an employee for reporting violations of the laws that the employer is included in. Unions are still exempt. Why?

The Heritage Foundation urgently demands: "Union employees need whistle-blower protections as much as employees of other organizations. The union movement is itself a big business. Labor unions collected an estimated $14 billion in dues and other assessments in 2010. Union officials have a fiduciary responsibility to use this money for the sole benefit of the union and its members. Union members may sue their union for breach of this fiduciary duty."

The book "Solidarity for sale – How corruption destroyed the labor movement and undermined America's promise" by Robert Fitch explains the dramatic situation perfectly.

In addition, labor law violations are not rare among the unions. According to the National Labor Relations Board, this is the current status:

1. Unfair Labor Practices filed against unions in the last 10 years: 78,903
2. The duty of Fair Representation 15,423
3. Hiring Halls 1,038
4. Union Security Related (including Beck) 641
5. Hiring Hall Related 606
6. Coercive Statements 525

We must be aware of the fact that unions themselves are "big business". Their annual membership fees reach or exceed 8.5 billion dollars per year. Let's not stop watching them carefully!

How to get rid of corrupt entitlements

Don't be surprised: Entitlements reach two-thirds of our national budget. It's much more than any other big government such as military or even the exploding public employee budget.

Even though the Social Security and Medicare cannot be considered as pure entitlements, they are in their current structure unsustainable. All political efforts to reform them have failed because Democrats don't want to touch Social Security or Medicare under any circumstances.

At this time, there is no political will and courage to tackle this giant national problem. With no realistic, market-oriented reform coming up soon, this is a time-bomb exploding no later than in the next decade.

Truth is that about half of Americans rely on some kind of handouts. Nobody really thinks that he or she is the problem. Only "others". As long as we think everything is another people's problem, nothing will change.

Our entitlement mindset is by far more dramatic than we think. Nobody wants to give up the "free stuff" – just the opposite.
The left is now propagating expanding the entitlements to a series of new free benefits such as free college tuition and even universal minimum income for everybody, independent from citizenship status and other factors.

Who is going to pay for that? "The rich", but they already pay the majority of taxes we mostly use for social experiments like entitlements. There is no tax base in the world that would be enough for such utopian measures. It's getting worse, and there is no end in sight.

Nobody argues that we must end all or most of our entitlements programs. The problem, however, is that all of them reached a proportion not sustainable in the future at all. If this continues, we'll face national bankruptcy sooner than we might think.

The major exploding entitlements programs are:

1. TANF – Temporary Assistance for Needy Families called welfare.
2. Medicaid serving over 60 million people.
3. CHIP – Child's Healthcare Insurance Program acting in addition to Medicaid and serving over 5 million children.
4. SNAP – Supplemental Nutrition Assistance Program commonly called Food stamps. The cost varies but often goes close to 100 billion per year.
5. Supplemental Security Program to help with cash to the aged, blind or disabled.
6. Earned Income Tax Credit for families with at least one child.
7. Housing Assistance Program mostly called Section 8 program. The assistance serves over 2 million renters.
8. LIHEAP or Low-Income home energy assistance program helping several million people.

The above list of entitlements programs is by far not complete. The Catalog of the Federal Domestic Assistance altogether lists over 1,600 federal funding programs published on AidPage by IDILOGIC. The total funding goes into trillions!

Every attempt to cut entitlements programs is called unethical and immoral by the left. However, we must face the facts. Here is an example, R. Bruce Josten, Exec. VP of Government Affairs at the US Chamber of Commerce, compiled together:

1. Entitlements programs are huge, very expensive and reach into every corner of our life.
2. Entitlements are no self-funding and are the main driver of our deficits.
3. Entitlements are growing at an alarming rate.
4. Longer life expectancy and changing demographics are the main reason that they are unsustainable.
5. Not one single major entitlement program is projected to be financially solvent in 20 years from now.
6. The projected cost of making entitlements programs in 75 years is calculated at 40 trillion.
7. The mandatory spending alone is already squeezing out important future investments.
8. Carefully-crafted phased-in adjustments are doable and over-due.
9. Reforms are possible without baseline cuts for nation's seniors, poor and disabled.
10. The biggest threat to our Social Security is doing nothing at all.

Reforming our entitlement system is one of the most monumental tasks of our time. Here too, there is no silver bullet in sight. Any reform must include fixes, adjustments and efficiency calculations. Here are some general guidelines:

1. We must contain our healthcare cost.
2. We must include free-market solutions like private savings.

3. We must consider the factor of our economic growth.

First of all, we must initiate an honest conversation based on truth and political, social and economic reality.

What do we have to watch for?

1. Wide-spread welfare fraud
2. Welfare for illegal aliens
3. Free college tuition for illegals
4. Out-of-control government spending
5. Outrageous entitlements for elected politicians

How to end the generational theft

Generational theft is a direct or indirect "stealing" money, services or other goods from one generation to another. Millions of millennials feel that they are being robbed by baby boomers. Is this true?

Generational theft is a systematic set of policies paying for current, often unsustainable projects at the expense of future economic stability and prosperity. This reaches from Social Security, Medicare, Medicaid to countless welfare programs such as housing assistance and more.

The argument is not that these expenses are morally and politically completely unnecessary. The big problem is only that they are not affordable and financed through debt paid for by future generations. That's why we call it generational theft.

The problem is especially visible by considering our completely unmanageable and unjust national debt. Our baby boomers went through some of the best time in America. Life was good for them in virtually all respects.

Now, they don't want to give their wealth and benefits up. Economists say, at the expense of their own children and grandchildren. They created a debt crisis nobody knows how to solve.

1. Liabilities that will take generations to repay
2. Safety nets for them none of their kids will ever be able to afford
3. Healthcare that does not pay for itself
4. Other entitlements our grandchildren will have to pay for

Many people also argue that our short-term-fix policies are unnecessarily adding to our debt and therefore contributing to the generational theft. Because of the never before seen polarization of our political process, not much of a wise long-term planning is doable in Washington.

How to establish government accountability

One of the major reasons of mistrust in public government is the widespread lack of accountability. If a CEO of a corporation commits major mistakes or improprieties, it usually doesn't take more than a few days to face consequences. He is fired or must resign.

In virtually all public administrations, the opposite is the case. The bad guys are covered by "solidarity". The cases against them are swept under the rug, nobody is held accountable. At the very best, the perpetrators get a slap on the wrist. It is mind-boggling!

How can we create a culture of accountability in our government? Here are some examples how to get started:

1. Elect or hire value-driven leaders only
2. Provide ethics training

3. Provide written policies and procedures
4. Consider an independent ethics commission
5. Demand accountability audits

The Project on Government oversight is trying to usher a new era in government accountability. Large government administrations are very complex entities and therefore very vulnerable to mismanagement and undue influence. Proper checks and balances are the only way to ensure an effective and ethical operation. We must keep the pressure. Fortunately, President Trump intends to improve the accountability through measures such as:

1. Setting and enforcement high standards in government ethics
2. Improvement of whistleblower protection laws
3. Establishment of a White House position focusing exclusively on transparency and accountability
4. Filling all Inspector General's positions
5. Ending secret laws
6. Practicing pro-active disclosures
7. Improvement of regulatory transparency
8. Strengthening of the Freedom of Information Act (FOIA)

How to expand right-to-work policies

The "right to work" principle demands that every American worker has the right to work for living without being compelled to belong to a union. While everybody should also have the right to join any union, nobody shall be forced to do so.

The National Right to Work Committee has close to three million members and defies the mandatory union membership for US workers. It appears that forcing Americans to bankroll the political advocacy of the unions is not constitutional.

According to the committee, current labor laws, as interpreted by federal courts, authorize the firing of private and public employees for refusal to pay for unwanted monopoly bargaining, unless the employees are protected by a Right to Work statute or state constitutional amendment.

The Heritage Foundation argues: "Mandatory dues hurt workers doubly. It forces them to pay for representation and political activities they may not want. It also makes unions less responsive to their interests. With mandatory dues, unions do not have to earn workers' support—they are compelled to provide it. Not surprisingly, unions charge higher dues and pay their officers higher salaries when workers have no choice but to pay."

Right to work laws make union membership voluntary and cause unions to work harder to earn worker's support. A Gallup polling finds that Americans support right-to-work by a three-to-one margin. The unions are fighting tooth and nail to defeat the right to work policies politically and legally.

Here is a short summary of all major facts about the right-to-work policy:

1. Makes union dues voluntary
2. Obliges unions to earn worker's support
3. Unions voluntarily support non-members
4. Unions usually spend little on representation
5. Companies consider it a major factor where to locate
6. Workers have the same buying power
7. Americans overwhelmingly support it

How to fight global warming fraud

Weather is changing all the time for thousands of years. "Climate change" has been rebranded from "global warming" because of the failure to prove the actual "warming."

Weather patterns always change. There is nothing unusual, alarming or perilous about it. This the beginning of the big deception. They call it climate change because nobody can deny that the weather changes all the time, but deceive people by denying this is natural.

Whatever political or societal puzzle you are researching, try investigating the "follow the money trail" first. Who is getting rich by promoting the global warming ideology?

1. First, "green investors" such as Al Gore are beneficiaries of his ideology
2. Secondly, all "green companies" such as now-bankrupt Solyndra that got over a half billion in government funds to promote "green alternatives" but terribly failed
3. Finally, scientists who can only get millions of research funds if they commit to advances to results the green lobby wants.

Let's be honest. There are some heavily conflicting facts we must face. While the global warming lobby wants us to believe that 97% of scientist believe that "human activity" is a significant factor in changing global temperatures, thousands of scientists document that "there is no convincing evidence" for that at all. What are we supposed to believe?

How to fight UN's green agenda

The "Intergovernmental Panel on Climate Change", the world's top scientific group dedicated to climate, published a paper that contains some of the most strident language yet by the panel about climate change.

UN states that "continued emission of greenhouse gases will cause further warming and long-lasting changes in all components of the climate system, increasing the likelihood of severe, pervasive and irreversible impacts on people and ecosystems."

It also warns that "human influence on the climate system is clear, and recent anthropogenic (man-made) emissions of greenhouse gases are the highest in history. The atmosphere and ocean have warmed, the amounts of snow and ice have diminished, and sea level has risen."

The UN's catastrophic conclusion: Earth is on its way to its hottest year ever recorded, along with its highest level of atmospheric carbon dioxide in at least 800,000 years. What? How do they know that?

If they can't prove it, it's speculation, and speculations are by no means facts. Interestingly, many UN "climate scientists" are not scientists at all, they are just politicians or green, Marxist-style activists.

The world's green lobby wants us to accept that their verdict is "final" and any deviation from their theory is anti-science and must be forbidden. Since when do we consider anything in science absolutely "final"?

All discoveries are at best "current research status" until a new research breaks new ground. By the way, the flat-earth theory was considered "final" for hundreds of years.

Even worse: Many of their agitators propose that "global warming deniers" like you and me should be criminalized.

Never has anything been so politicized and radicalized as the global warming theory today.

How to publicize the global warming hoax

Among many specific studies, one of the world's top meteorology research institutions found that our atmosphere might be "much less sensitive to carbon dioxide emissions than we think".

The Max Planck Institute for Meteorology in Germany found that man-made aerosols make a much smaller effect on the atmosphere than theoretical computer models of the green lobby suggest.

The study says that the carbon in the atmosphere in fact "deflects" the sun – and therefore leads to more cooling than anticipated. Aerosols are produced by human activities like burning coal, driving cars or other fires. Natural aerosols are also clouds and fog. They even reflect the sun into space and offset any kind of warming by CO2 emissions.

Truth is that most scientists, adhering to the green agenda often use inappropriate scientific data. They pick and choose what to include and what not to include. They use computer models, but they can only respond to the data they have been fed.

How a Nobel laureate describes global warming: Pseudo-science

Nobel laureate in physics, Professor Ivar Giaever, calls global warming studies presented by the world's green lobby "Pseudo-Science." The physicist says global warming is a new religion of the left. They don't believe in God, they don't believe in the Bible – they just believe in their Marxist ideology.

Global warming theory is just what they need to enact government control over energy. And as Stalin and Hitler said, who controls a nation's energy, also controls a nation's industrial production, job market, and politics.

In other words, it's not about the climate and "saving the world", it is about political and economic power. This is perfectly in agreement with the Marxist worldview and communist manifesto.

Like socialists are never allowing to question their worldview or to contradict their ideology, "green scientists" and green politicians also don't allow any discussion. Al Gore demanded years ago, that the "scientific consensus on global warming is settled and we must stop discussing and questioning his claim."

In science, nothing is ever "settled" for the rest of our time. Any new discovery might overthrow the old one, this is research principle 101. Thousands of scientific discoveries have been overturned during the last hundreds of years.

How the global warming hysteria is "cult science"

The more we watch and discuss the global warming hysteria, no rational, common sense, truth-based idea is applicable. No normal discussion, no criticism, no challenging scientific data is permitted. As Al Gore said, the verdict is final. No more discussion. Is the science settled? Leading psychologists say that the global warming worldview is a religion – or better yet a cult.

The cult of global warming is unfortunately not exclusively limited to left-wing zealots. Some traditional "group thinkers" became victims of this purpose-agenda. Cult leaders like Al Gore don't allow any objection to their philosophy. Like in the middle ages: shoot the messenger.

Donald Trump requested an objective scientific investigation of the hysteria and stopped wasting billions of dollars on highly questionable "green" projects. Of course, Trump's logical, business-type free-market approach is an existential threat to Marxism and their green-red agenda.

One of the most frequent arguments the left has is that global warming skepticism is "anti-science." The opposite in fact is true. More and more scientific studies have come out destroying climate alarmists claim.

How and why the climate change is natural

The European Foundation issued a dossier explaining why climate change is a natural phenomenon and not a man-made one. They cite one hundred reasons why.

1. There is "no real scientific proof" that the current warming is caused by the rise of greenhouse gases from man's activity.

2. Man-made carbon dioxide emissions throughout human history constitute less than 0.00022 percent of the total naturally emitted from the mantle of the earth during geological history.

3. Warmer periods of the Earth's history came around 800 years before rises in CO2 levels.

4. After World War II, there was a huge surge in recorded CO2 emissions, but global temperatures fell for four decades after 1940.

5. Throughout the Earth's history, temperatures have often been warmer than now and CO2 levels have often been higher – more than ten times as high.

6. Significant changes have continually occurred throughout geologic time.

7. The 0.7C increase in the average global temperature over the last hundred years is entirely consistent with well-established, long-term, natural climate trends.

8. The IPCC theory is driven by just 60 scientists and favourable reviewers, not the 4,000 usually cited.

9. Leaked e-mails from British climate scientists in a scandal known as "Climate-gate" suggest that they were manipulated to exaggerate global warming.

10. A large body of scientific research suggests that the sun is responsible for the greater share of climate change during the past hundred years.

11. Politicians and activists claim rising sea levels are a direct cause of global warming, but sea level rates have been increasing steadily since the last ice age 10,000 years ago.

12. Philip Stott, Emeritus Professor of Biogeography at the School of Oriental and African Studies in London, says climate change is too complicated to be caused by just one factor, whether CO2 or clouds.

13. Peter Lilley, MP said that "fewer people in Britain than in any other country believe in the importance of global warming. That is despite the fact that our Government and predominantly our political class are more committed to it than their counterparts in any other country in the world".

14. In pursuit of the global warming rhetoric, wind farms will do very little to nothing to reduce CO2 emissions.

15. Professor Plimer, heading Geology and Earth Sciences at the University of Adelaide, stated that the idea of taking a single trace gas in the atmosphere, accusing it and finding it guilty of total responsibility for climate change, is an "absurdity".

16. A Harvard University astrophysicist and geophysicist, Willie Soon, said he is "embarrassed and puzzled" by the shallow science in papers that support the proposition that the earth faces a climate crisis caused by global warming.

17. The science of what determines the earth's temperature is in fact far from settled or understood/

18. Despite activist concerns over CO2 levels, CO2 is a minor greenhouse gas, unlike water vapor which is tied to climate concerns, and which we can't even pretend to control.

19. A petition by scientists trying to tell the world that the political and media portrayal of global warming is false was put forward in the Heidelberg Appeal in 1992. Today, more than 4,000 signatories, including 72 Nobel Prize winners, from 106 countries have signed it.

20. It is claimed the average global temperature increased at a dangerously fast rate in the 20th century, but the recent rate of average global temperature rise has been between 1 and 2 degrees C per century - within natural rates.

21. Professor Zbigniew Jaworowski, Chairman of the Scientific Council of the Central Laboratory for Radiological Protection in Warsaw, Poland, says the earth's temperature has more to do with cloud cover and water vapor than the CO2 concentration in the atmosphere.

22. There is strong evidence from solar studies that suggest that the Earth's current temperature stasis will be followed by climatic cooling over the next few decades.

23. It is a myth that receding glaciers are proof of global warming as glaciers have been receding and growing cyclically for many centuries.

24. It is a falsehood that the earth's poles are warming because that is a natural variation and while the western Arctic may be getting somewhat warmer, we also see that the Eastern Arctic and Greenland are getting colder.

25. The IPCC claims climate driven "impacts on biodiversity are significant and of key relevance," but those claims are simply not supported by scientific research.

26. The IPCC threat of climate change to the world's species does not make sense as wild species are at least one million years old, which means they have all been through hundreds of climate cycles.

27. Research goes strongly against claims that CO2-induced global warming would cause catastrophic disintegration of the Greenland and Antarctic ice sheets.

28. Despite activist concerns over CO2 levels, rising CO2 levels are our best hope of raising crop yields to feed an ever-growing population.

29. The biggest climate change ever experienced on earth took place around 700 million years ago.

30. The slight increase in temperature, which has been observed since 1900, is entirely consistent with well-established, long-term natural climate cycles.

31. Despite activist concerns over CO2 levels, rising CO2 levels of some so-called "greenhouse gases" may be contributing to higher oxygen levels and global cooling, not warming.

32. Accurate satellite, balloon and mountain top observations made over the last three decades have not shown any significant change in the long-term rate of increase in global temperatures.

33. Today's CO2 concentration of around 385 ppm is very low compared to most of the earth's history. We actually live in a carbon-deficient atmosphere.

34. It is a myth that CO2 is the most common greenhouse gas because greenhouse gases form about 3% of the atmosphere by volume, and CO2 constitutes about 0.037% of the atmosphere.

35. It is a myth that computer models verify that CO2 increases will cause significant global warming because computer models can be made to "verify" anything

36. There is no scientific or statistical evidence whatsoever that global warming will cause more storms and other weather extremes.

37. One statement deleted from a UN report in 1996 stated that "none of the studies cited above have shown clear evidence that we can attribute the observed climate changes to increases in greenhouse gases".

38. The world "warmed" by 0.07 +/- 0.07 degrees C from 1999 to 2008, not the 0.20 degrees C expected by the IPCC.

39. The Intergovernmental Panel on Climate Change says "it is likely that future tropical cyclones (typhoons and hurricanes) will become more intense," but there has been no increase in the intensity or frequency of tropical cyclones globally.

40. Rising CO2 levels in the atmosphere can be shown not only to have a negligible effect on the Earth's many ecosystems but in some cases to be a positive help to many organisms.

41. Researchers who compare and contrast climate change impact on civilizations found warm periods are beneficial to mankind and cold periods harmful.

42. The Met Office asserts we are in the hottest decade since records began, but this is precisely what the world should expect if the climate is cyclical.

43. Rising CO2 levels increase plant growth and make plants more resistant to drought and pests.

44. The historical increase in the air's CO2 content has improved human nutrition by raising crop yields during the past 150 years.

45. The increase of the air's CO2 content has probably helped lengthen human lifespans since the beginning of the Industrial Revolution.

46. The IPCC alleges that "climate change currently contributes to the global burden of disease and premature deaths," but the evidence shows that higher temperatures and rising CO2 levels have helped global populations.

47. In May of 2004, the Russian Academy of Sciences published a report concluding that the Kyoto Protocol has no scientific grounding at all.

48. The "Climate-gate" scandal pointed to an expensive public campaign of disinformation and the denigration of scientists who opposed the belief that CO2 emissions were causing climate change.

49. The head of Britain's climate change watchdog has predicted households will need to spend up to £15,000 on a full energy efficiency makeover if the Government is to meet its ambitious targets for cutting carbon emissions.

50. Wind power is unlikely to be the answer to our energy needs. The wind power industry argues that there are "no direct subsidies," but it involves a total subsidy of as much as £60 per MWh, which falls directly on electricity consumers. This burden will grow in line with attempts to achieve Wind power targets, according to a recent OFGEM report.

51. Wind farms are not an efficient way to produce energy. The British Wind Energy Association (BWEA) accepts a figure of 75 percent backup power is required.

52. Global temperatures are below the low end of IPCC predictions not "at the top end of IPCC estimates".

53. Climate alarmists have raised the concern over acidification of the oceans, but Tom Segalstad from Oslo University in Norway and others have noted that the composition of ocean water – including CO2, calcium, and water – can act as a buffering agent in the acidification of the oceans.

54. The UN's IPCC computer models of human-caused global warming predict the emergence of a "hotspot" in the upper troposphere over the tropics. Former researcher in the Australian Department of Climate Change, David Evans, said there is no evidence of such a hotspot.

55. The argument that climate change is a result of global warming caused by human activity is the argument of "flat-earthers".

56. The manner in which US President Barack Obama sidestepped Congress to order emission cuts shows how undemocratic and irrational the entire international decision-making process has become with regards to emission-target setting/

57. William Kininmonth, a former head of the National Climate Centre and a consultant to the World Meteorological Organization, wrote "the likely extent of global temperature rise from a doubling of CO2 is less than 1C. Such warming is well within the envelope of variation experienced during the past 10,000 years and insignificant in the context of glacial cycles during the past million years when the earth has been predominantly very cold and covered by extensive ice sheets."

58. Canada has shown that the world targets derived
    from the existing Kyoto commitments were
    always unrealistic and did not work for the
    country.

59. In the lead up to the Copenhagen summit, David
    Davis, MP, said of previous climate summits, at
    Rio de Janeiro in 1992 and Kyoto in 1997 that
    many had promised greater cuts, but "neither
    happened", but we are continuing along the same
    lines.

60. The UK 's environmental policy has a long-term
    price tag of about £55 billion, before considering
    the impact on its economic growth.

61. The UN's panel on climate change warned that
    Himalayan glaciers could melt to a fifth of current
    levels by 2035. J. Graham Cogley, a professor at
    Ontario Trent University, claims this is inaccurate
    stating the UN authors got the date from an earlier
    report wrong by more than 300 years.

62. Under existing Kyoto obligations, the EU has
    attempted to claim success, while actually
    increasing emissions by 13 percent, according to
    Lord Lawson. In addition, the EU has pursued this
    scheme by purchasing "offsets" from countries
    such as China paying them billions of dollars to
    destroy atmospheric pollutants, such as CFC-23,
    which were manufactured purely in order to be
    destroyed.

63. It is claimed that the average global temperature
    was relatively unchanging in pre-industrial times
    but sky-rocketed since 1900, and will increase by
    several degrees more over the next 100 years
    according to Penn State University researcher
    Michael Mann. There is no convincing empirical

evidence that past climate was unchanging, nor that 20th-century changes in average global temperature were unusual or unnatural.

64. Michael Mann of Penn State University has actually shown that the Medieval Warm Period and the Little Ice Age did in fact exist, which contrasts with his earlier work which produced the "hockey stick graph" showing a constant temperature over the past thousand years or so followed by a recent dramatic upturn.

65. The globe's current approach to climate change in which major industrialized countries agreed to nonsensical targets for their CO2 emissions by a given date, as it has been under the Kyoto system, is very expensive.

66. The "Climate-gate" scandal revealed that a scientific team had emailed one another about using a "trick" for the sake of concealing a "decline" in temperatures when looking at the history of the earth's temperature.

67. Global temperatures have not risen in any statistically significant sense for 15 years and have actually been falling for nine years. The "Climate-gate" scandal revealed a scientific team had expressed dismay at the fact global warming was contrary to their predictions and admitted their inability to explain it was "a travesty".

68. The IPCC predicts that a warmer planet will lead to more extreme weather, including drought, flooding, storms, snow, and wildfires. But over the last century, during which the IPCC claims the world experienced more rapid warming than any time in the past two millennia, the world did not

experience significantly greater trends in any of these extreme weather events.

69. In explaining the average temperature standstill we are currently experiencing, the Met Office Hadley Centre ran a series of computer climate predictions and found in many of the computers runs there were decade-long standstills but none for 15 years, so it expects global warming to resume swiftly.

70. Richard Lindzen, professor of Atmospheric Sciences at Massachusetts Institute of Technology, wrote: "The notion of a static, unchanging climate is foreign to the history of the Earth or any other planet with a fluid envelope. Such hysteria over global warming simply represents the scientific illiteracy of much of the public and the susceptibility of the public to the substitution of repetition for truth.

71. Despite the 1997 Kyoto Protocol's status as the flagship of the fight against climate change, it has been a failure.

72. The first phase of the EU's Emissions Trading Scheme (ETS) which ran from 2005 to 2007 was a failure. Huge over-allocation of permits to pollute led to a collapse in the price of carbon from €33 to just €0.20 per ton meaning the system did not reduce emissions at all.

73. The EU trading scheme to manage carbon emissions has completely failed and actually allows European businesses to duck out of making their emission reductions at home by offsetting, which means paying for cuts to be made overseas instead

74. To date "cap and trade" carbon markets have done almost nothing to reduce emissions.

75. In the United States, the cap-and-trade is an approach designed to control carbon emissions and will impose huge costs upon American citizens via a carbon tax on all goods and services produced in the United States. The average family of four can expect to pay an additional $1700, or £1,043, more each year. It is predicted that the United States will lose more than 2 million jobs as a result of cap-and-trade schemes.

76. Dr. Roy Spencer, a principal research scientist at the University of Alabama in Huntsville, has indicated that out of the 21 climate models tracked by the IPCC, the differences in warming exhibited by those models is mostly the result of different strengths of positive cloud feedback, and that increasing CO_2 is insufficient to explain global-average warming in the last 50 to 100 years.

77. Why should politicians devote our scarce resources in a globally competitive world to a false and ill-defined problem, while ignoring the real problems the entire planet faces, such as poverty, hunger, disease or terrorism?

78. A proper analysis of ice core records from the past 650,000 years demonstrates that temperature increases have come before, and have not resulted from increases in CO_2 by hundreds of years.

79. Since the cause of global warming is primarily natural, then it's actual fact that it is very little we can do about it. We are still not able to control the sun.

80. A substantial number of the panel of 2,500 climate scientists on the United Nation's International Panel on Climate Change, which created a statement on scientific unanimity on climate change and man-made global warming, were found to have serious concerns.

81. The UK's Met Office has been forced this year to re-examine 160 years of temperature data after admitting that public confidence in the science on man-made global warming has been shattered by revelations about the data.

82. Politicians and activists push for renewable energy sources such as wind turbines under the rhetoric of climate change, but it is essentially about money – under the system of Renewable Obligations. Consumers in electricity bills pay much of the cost for, amounting to £1 billion a year.

83. The "Climate-gate" scandal revealed that a scientific team had tampered with their own data so as to conceal inconsistencies and errors.

84. The "Climate-gate" scandal revealed that a scientific team had campaigned for the removal of a learned journal's editor, solely because he did not share their willingness to debase science for political purposes.

85. Ice-core data clearly show that temperatures change centuries before concentrations of atmospheric CO2 change. Thus, there appears to be little evidence for insisting that changes in concentrations of CO2 are the cause of past temperature and climate change.

86. There are no experimentally verified processes explaining how CO2 concentrations can fall in a

few centuries without falling temperatures. In fact, it is changing temperatures which cause changes in CO2 concentrations, which is consistent with experiments that show CO2 is the atmospheric gas most readily absorbed by water.

87. The Government's Renewable Energy Strategy contains a massive increase in electricity generation by wind power costing around £4 billion a year over the next twenty years. The benefits will be only £4 to £5 billion overall (not per annum). So costs will outnumber benefits by a range of between eleven and seventeen times.

88. Whilst CO2 levels have indeed changed for various reasons, human and otherwise, just as they have throughout history, the CO2 content of the atmosphere has increased since the beginning of the industrial revolution, and the growth rate has now been constant for the past 25 years.

89. It is a myth that CO2 is a pollutant because nitrogen forms 80% of our atmosphere and human beings could not live in 100% nitrogen either. CO2 is no more a pollutant than nitrogen is, and CO2 is essential to life.

90. Politicians and climate activists make claims to rising sea levels but certain members in the IPCC chose an area to measure in Hong Kong that is subsiding. They used the record reading of 2.3 mm per year rise of sea level.

91. The accepted global average temperature statistics used by the Intergovernmental Panel on Climate Change show that no ground-based warming has occurred since 1998.

92. If one factor in non-greenhouse influences such as El Nino events and large volcanic eruptions, lower atmosphere satellite-based temperature measurements show little, if any, global warming since 1979, a period over which atmospheric CO2 has increased by 55 ppm (17 percent).

93. US President Barack Obama pledged to cut emissions by 2050 to equal those of 1910 when there were 92 million Americans. In 2050, there will be 420 million Americans, so Obama's promise means that emissions per head will be approximately what they were in 1875. It simply will not happen.

94. The European Union has already agreed to cut emissions by 20 percent by 2020, compared with 1990 levels and is willing to increase the target to 30 percent. However, these are unachievable, and the EU has already massively failed with its Emissions Trading Scheme (ETS), as EU emissions actually rose by 0.8 percent from 2005 to 2006 and are known to be well above the Kyoto goal.

95. Australia has stated it wants to slash greenhouse emissions by up to 25 percent below 2000 levels by 2020, but the pledges were so unpopular that the country's Senate has voted against the carbon trading bill, and a climate change sceptic has now ousted the Opposition's Party leader.

96. Canada plans to reduce emissions by 20 percent compared with 2006 levels by 2020, representing approximately a 3 percent cut from 1990 levels, but it simultaneously defends its Alberta tar sands emissions and its record as one of the world's highest per-capita emissions setters.

97. India plans to reduce the ratio of emissions to production by 20-25 percent compared with 2005 levels by 2020, but all Government officials insist that since India has to grow for its development and poverty alleviation, it has to emit because the economy is driven by carbon.

98. The Leipzig Declaration in 1996 was signed by 110 scientists who said: "We – along with many of our fellow citizens – are apprehensive about the climate treaty conference scheduled in Kyoto, Japan, in December 1997" and "based on all the evidence available to us, we cannot subscribe to the politically inspired world view that envisages climate catastrophes and calls for hasty actions."

99. A US Oregon Petition Project stated: "We urge the United States government to reject the global warming agreement that was written in Kyoto, Japan in December 1997, and any other similar proposals. The proposed limits on greenhouse gases would harm the environment, hinder the advance of science and technology, and damage the health and welfare of mankind. There is no convincing scientific evidence that human release of CO_2, methane, or other greenhouse gasses is causing or will in the foreseeable future cause catastrophic heating of the earth's atmosphere and disruption of the Earth's climate."

100. A report by the Nongovernmental International Panel on Climate Change concluded: "We find no support for the IPCC's claim that climate observations during the twentieth century are either unprecedented or provide evidence of an anthropogenic effect on climate."

This compilation of facts is several years old. Meanwhile, countless additional studies have proven that the climate change claim is basically a politically motivated scientific fraud.

Proponents of the global warming ideology cite a very questionable poll suggesting that 97% of "scientists" asked claim that global warming is man-made. First of all, a poll is not a proof for a theory, just an opinion poll.

Secondly, how many of them are real climatologists and not just activists working in different of scientific fields not related to earth sciences?

More reliable is the statement by the NAS (National Association of Scholars) indicating that at least forty percent of scientists doubt global warming.

The probably worst part is that virtually all climate researchers are forced into group thinking. There are almost no public funds available anywhere in the world for independent climate change research.

Practically all research funds available are expected only "to prove" global warming – and not to investigate the problem scientifically. The scientists depending on public research funds have no choice but to commit to the global warming hoax before they receive one penny.

Altogether, the climate change hoax has more holes than the Swiss cheese. Let's use the holes to beat them!

How to avoid UN takeover

UN is no friend of the US and certainly no fan of democracy, freedom or personals liberty. One of the most dangerous but hardly known anti-American actions is the United Nations' Agenda 21. This is theoretically legally a "non-binding, voluntary implemented action plan of the UN with regard to sustainable development…"

In reality, it is a broad Marxist worldview policy forced on American people with disastrous consequences for the American way of life.

The sneakiest part is the "Local governments for sustainability project" founded by the UN "International Council for Local Initiatives." It includes about 1,300 local governments in 70 countries and it is growing rapidly. We must take action.

The UN tries to co-opt with local governments with the end goal of "one-world-government". The privately held land will be eliminated to ensure "sustainability" via depopulation and population control.

Theoretically, the UN just provides "technical consulting, training and information services to build capacity, share knowledge and support local governments in the implementation of sustainable development."

In reality, the terrible consequence of that is this UN measure infringes on our property rights and forces a radical green agenda on everybody in the world.

Of course, such extremist one-world-government agendas clash drastically with our Constitution and our Bill of Rights. This is not new. A report from a 1976 UN conference in Vancouver, British Columbia, on human settlements, lays out the scary position today embraced by most Democrats who also don't hide the actual intent anymore:

1. "Land cannot be treated as an ordinary asset, controlled by individuals and subject to the pressures and inefficiencies of the market.

2. "Private land ownership is also a principal instrument of accumulation and concentration of wealth and therefore contributes to social injustice; if unchecked, it may become a major obstacle in the planning and implementation of development schemes."

3. "The provision of decent dwellings and healthy conditions for the people can only be achieved if the land is used in the interest of society as a whole."

We were able to fight back: After major protests by concerned citizens and conservative organizations, during the last months, a series of US cities and towns began withdrawing from their UN agenda participation. Still, many Marxism-oriented cities in America are happily continuing with Agenda 21.

Virtually everything is extremely alarming. One aspect of Agenda 21 is a "human settlement" objective in order to "improve the social, economic and environmental quality" of the world. Their special focus is on special groups such as women, indigenous people, elderly and disabled. The UN plan includes:

1. Providing adequate shelter for all people
2. Improving human settlement management
3. Promoting sustainable land-use planning and management

4. Providing integrated provisions of environmental structure for water, sanitation, drainage and solid-waste management
5. Promoting sustainable energy and transport systems in human settlements
6. Promoting human settlement planning and management in disaster-prone areas
7. Promoting sustainable construction industry activities
8. Promoting human resource development and capacity-building for human settlement development

The UN practically demands: All governments shall create "appropriate provisions" to monitor the impact of UN strategies on "marginalized and disenfranchised" groups in accordance with their worldview.

As good as the measures might sound for socialists, de facto it totally destroys personal property and individual freedoms worldwide. The danger is by far not over. We must continue to fight UN's socialist agenda.

Let's not forget which kind of countries dominate the UN. The vast majority of their member states are either communist, Muslim or otherwise totalitarian forces despising democracy, liberty, and personal freedom. We have nothing in common with them!

How to avoid a national security catastrophe

At the end of the Obama era, our national defense was in a desolate state. The size of our troops was smaller than at the end of WW2. The number or our ships reached the lowest point in fifty years. Many of our airplanes we fly to defend America were older than the pilots who fly them.

This did not happen by accident. As Obama admitted, again and again, a weak America will produce a more peaceful world. Therefore, Obama did not miss a point to weaken our military and destroy our defense readiness dramatically.

The catastrophic deteriorating of our defense capabilities came as a direct result of Obama's "do nothing" foreign policy rule. Not unlike Bill Clinton, his administration misjudged and mishandled almost everything:

1. Arab Spring
2. ISIS and the rise of Islamism
3. Benghazi
4. Afghanistan
5. Iraq
6. Syria
7. Iran
8. North Korea

How to rebuild our defense structure

House Speaker Paul Ryan summarized some of the catastrophic consequences of Obama's policies:

1. Politicizing our military
2. Blocking pay raise for our troops
3. Failing to invest in new hardware and equipment

4. Allowing Veterans Administration to fail the people they were supposed to serve

Hostile countries such as China, Russia, Iran, North Korea and other enemy powers are overtaking us in defense spending by a factor three to five. If we don't catch up to their arms race, we'll face a national security crisis of gigantic proportions.

We have no choice. When we can't defend ourselves sufficiently anymore, our days are numbered.

Thank God, the Trump administration understands the problem and is taking swift action. According to President Trump, our national security strategy consists of the following four pillars:

1. Protection of the homeland
2. Promotion of the American prosperity
3. Peace preservation through military strength
4. Advancement of US influence

Our official strategy addresses key challenges and trends that affect our standing in the world, including:

1. Revisionist powers, such as China and Russia, that use technology, propaganda, and coercion to shape a world antithetical to our interests and values;

2. Regional dictators that spread terror, threaten their neighbors, and pursue weapons of mass destruction;

3. Jihadist terrorists that foment hatred to incite violence against innocents in the name of a wicked ideology, and transnational criminal organizations that spill drugs and violence into our communities.

Trump's strategy articulates and advances the President's concept of principled realism.

1. It is realistic because it acknowledges the central role of power in international politics, affirms that strong and sovereign states are the best hope for a peaceful world, and clearly defines our national interests.

2. It is principled because it is grounded in advancing American principles, which spreads peace and prosperity around the globe.

Our national defense shall strengthen control of our borders and reform our immigration system to protect the homeland and restore our sovereignty. According to the White House, the greatest transnational threats to the homeland are:

1. Jihadist terrorists, using barbaric cruelty to commit murder, repression, and slavery, and virtual networks to exploit vulnerable populations and inspire and direct plots.

2. Transnational criminal organizations, tearing apart our communities with drugs and violence and weakening our allies and partners by corrupting democratic institutions.

As the President promised, America will target threats at their source. The US will confront threats before they ever reach our borders or cause harm to our people.

America will redouble our efforts to protect our critical infrastructure and digital networks because new technology and new adversaries create new vulnerabilities.

Our military officials are deploying a layered missile defense system to defend America against missile attacks.

128

Strengthening our national defense is a very complex issue. It does not just mean more soldiers, better weapons, and more sophisticated strategy. This also means economic prosperity in America because only a prosperous country can afford the defense budget we badly need.

1. We need to rejuvenate the American economy for the benefit of American workers and companies, which is necessary to restore our national power.

2. America cannot any longer tolerate chronic trade abuses and will pursue free, fair, and reciprocal economic relationships.

3. In order to succeed in this 21st-century geopolitical competition, America must lead in research, technology, and innovation. We will protect our national security innovation base from those who steal our intellectual property and unfairly exploit the innovation of free societies.

4. America must use its energy dominance to ensure international markets remain open, and that the benefits of diversification and energy access promote economic and national security.

The only approach to our national security is what Ronald Reagan enacted: peace through strength. No weak country can endure peace and freedom. The best peace insurance is always our own military power.

1. We need to rebuild America's military strength to ensure it remains second to none.

2. We must use all of the tools of statecraft in a new era of strategic competition—diplomatic, information, military, and economic—to protect our interests.

3. We shall strengthen our capabilities across numerous domains — including space and cyber — and revitalize capabilities that have been neglected.

4. We supposed to motivate our allies and partners to magnify our power and protect our shared interests. We expect them to take greater responsibility for addressing common threats.

5. We must guarantee that the balance of power remains in America's favor in key regions of the world: the Indo-Pacific, Europe, and the Middle East.

When America is weak, the entire world is weak. We don't look for our role as "world policeman", but without our interventions, everything goes south. This is especially true because the UN is in most areas of world trouble virtually useless. If we don't advance humanity, nobody will!

1. We must continue to enhance our influence overseas to protect the American people and promote our prosperity.

2. America's diplomatic and development efforts will compete to achieve better outcomes in all arenas—bilateral, multilateral, and in the information realm—to protect our interests, find new economic opportunities for Americans, and challenge our competitors.

3. America must seek partnerships with like-minded states to promote free market economies, private sector growth, political stability, and peace.

4. Americans champion our values – including the rule of law and individual rights – that promote strong, stable, prosperous, and sovereign states.

5. Our America First foreign policy celebrates America's influence in the world as a positive force that can help set the conditions for peace, prosperity, and the development of successful societies.

How to keep our defense state-of-the-art

Nobody doubts that we urgently need to modernize our entire defense system. This does not mean only new and additional weapons. This means that we need a completely new defense strategy, tactics, hardware, and software.

In some crucial areas, we are lagging badly behind Russia and China. This must change asap! DARPA (Defense Research Project Agency) is developing a number of measures to catch up with our enemies.

1. Testing more computers than weapons. DARPA is exploring a wide range of cybersecurity options and offensive capabilities. This includes a number of defensive and offensive software programs in beta stage.
2. The CORONET project investigates the technologies to dramatically ramp up internet speed in order to expedite the communications between different command centers. The civilian internet users might also profit from this measure.

3. Developing a huge, solar-based, self-sustaining atmospheric reconnaissance blimp. Practically, this is a stratospheric airship that should conduct persistent wide-area surveillance, tracking, and engagement of air and ground targets. It is also supposed to include a new generation of radar and be also used for weather forecast purposes.
4. A fixed wireless data system that would not slow down when they are crowded. The number of users will be able to grow without slowing it down.
5. Major improvement in the military communications system with speeds up to Gigabit per second.
6. Renewable-at-sea power program trying to convert ocean waves into energy. This should enable the application of underwater drones and automated underwater vehicles.
7. The thermal management system is searching for materials that can survive vast amounts of heat such as jet engines produce. Of course, such technology could be very useful for civilian purposes also.
8. Advanced radio mapping project is searching for better ways to avoid interferences and jamming by enemies.
9. The aero-optic beam control system is supposed to put a defensive laser into skies. It should arm aircraft with powerful lasers that can shoot backward.
10. They intend to re-think and re-imagine the way we share our web content.
11. Their "Visibuilding" program is also very ambitious and wants to "see" everything within building or structures from outside. It is supposed to provide full 3D maps of everything. This might be also very helpful for police or firefighter work.

12. Another new technology is meant to effectively but inexpensively provide a situational awareness and security in remote areas such as the Arctic. This technology too shall have countless scientific and commercial applications.
13. Offensive laser weapon on airplanes by their "High Energy Liquid Area Defense system" is supposed to enable airplanes to defend themselves against flying missiles.
14. Biofuel research that actually earned some criticism because being primarily political and does not seem to be economically and technically feasible.

How to prepare for an EMP attack

It is one the scariest weapons of mass destruction we can imagine. Despite that, most people don't know what it is and most politicians have disregarded it for decades: EMP, electromagnetic pulse, caused mostly by a nuclear device at a high altitude above us.

"A single nuclear weapon detonated at high altitude over this country would collapse our electrical grid and other critical infrastructures and endanger the lives of millions," a GOP platform stated. "With North Korea in possession of nuclear missiles and Iran close to having them, an EMP is no longer a theoretical concern—it is a real threat."

Former CIA Director James Wolsey said he believes that an EMP detonation above the US would cause millions of lives and the entire society to collapse. This major homeland security catastrophe threat still is widely ignored.

An EMP attack could irreparably cripple our country with not much chance of recovery. A successful attack on The US would have catastrophic consequences. There would be an immediate total and irreversible blackout and would destroy virtually everything essential to our survival:

1. All electronic systems
2. Electric grid system
3. Cars and trucks
4. Transportation
5. Airplanes
6. Railroads
7. Hospital equipment
8. All ignition systems
9. Medical equipment
10. Pacemakers
11. Communications systems
12. Road and rail signals
13. Industrial controls
14. Cell phones
15. Radio frequencies
16. Energy supply
17. Food supply
18. Water supply
19. Public services
20. And much more

With no food, water, transportation, and the help of any kind, most of the people would die within days or weeks. At this time, only a very few places such as the White House and major military installations are sufficiently protected against the EMP. This is an outrage!

The time is to act now. Contact your Senators and Representatives and demand action before it's too late. If all of our essential installations are properly shielded, most of the electrical and electronic devices can survive even the strongest EMP attack. According to some estimates, such a shielding of vital survival infrastructure should not cost much more than ten billion dollars. Compared to catastrophic consequences, this is a pocket change.

The Congress must urgently act and start implementing the following key measures:

1. Perform more wide-ranging research on the effect of the EMP and the following national security threat in general.
2. Build a comprehensive missile defense system in order to be able to shoot down incoming ballistic missiles.
3. Develop a national security plan incorporating the effects of an EMP attack identifying all key effects on our power grid, telecommunications, and other vital infrastructure areas.
4. Shielding of all vulnerable infrastructure areas such as defense and national security operations, power and water supply, traffic and communications centers and other key points vital for US survival.

For the first time, our Administration indeed listened to concerned people. The Dept. of Energy developed the "DOE Electromagnetic Pulse Resilience Plan" in cooperation with the Electric Power Research Institute. The final description now is "Joint Electromagnetic Pulse Resilience Strategy".

1. Improve and share the understanding of EMP: Threat, Effects, and impact
2. Identify priority infrastructure
3. Test and promote mitigation and protection approaches
4. Enhance response and recovery capabilities
5. Share best practices across the government and industry nationally and internationally

The complete Action Plan is available at the Dept. of Energy website.

How to stop nuclear Iran and N. Korea

One of the most difficult foreign and defense problems of the last fifty years is the nuclearizing of Iran and N. Korea. All options are on the table – and all are bad because they could initiate the WW3.

Still, we can't allow N. Korea to proceed and directly threaten us with nuclear annihilation. At the same time, it is absolutely essential that we stop Iran's nuclear ambitions threatening Israel and the entire Middle East region. What can we do?

There are no good options, and all are extremely difficult and dangerous. Only the smartest political and military minds might come to some may be acceptable solutions. The good thing is that Trump is not a collectivist type of politician. He is not a group thinker, he is an individualist who is able to think out-of-the-box.

First of all, nuclear weapons are for N. Korea and Iran the only survival guarantee. They will never give it up and use it, at best, as a bargaining chip. As we have seen in the past, all agreements with them weren't much more worth than the paper they were written on. They both lie, cheat and fool us as long as we don't catch up with their game.

Considering the seriousness of the situation, we must be aware where we stand now.

1. We are too late in the game for any good option
2. We must avoid the temptation to do nothing
3. We must extremely carefully calculate the dangers of a pre-emptive strike
4. We must do everything to engage China and convince them that N. Kore's nuclear power is not in their own interest

5. Trump's strategy brings new chances and some new risks

With Iran, the time is running out too. They are progressing rapidly with the development of nuclear warheads and ballistic missiles. As Iran's Muslim ruler Rouhani emphasized, Obama's nuclear deal with them "won't stop Iran to acquire nuclear weapons" they intend to use primarily to annihilate Israel.

Since there are no viable solutions in sight, most world leaders and Washington elitists promote the notion that "the Iran agreement is not good", but still the best way to "maintain peace and stability" in the region. Really?

The Carnegie Endowment for International Peace and the Center for a New American Security published a common paper that mostly welcomes Iran Agreement and encourages our government to use this opportunity to advance our position with mostly diplomatic means.

According to them, the Joint Comprehensive Plan of Action (JCPOA) accomplishes exactly what we had in mind: preventing Iran from developing a nuclear weapon. Who does still believe that?

The study paper lists a number of measures how to maintain and intelligently deal with status quo des agreements, focusing mostly on smart diplomacy and monitoring Iran's activities.

Unfortunately, we don't really know what Iran is doing because the JCPOA does not allow any really objective independent control of Iran's research and nuclear production. According to the study, we shall still "vigorously employ our verification tools" in the hope Iran complies. Did they ever do that?

1. Closely monitor Iran's nuclear program (in collaboration with friendly partners) to detect any indication of activity to acquire nuclear weapons or otherwise violate the JCPOA.

2. Work closely now with international counterparts to pre-plan for a coordinated, proportional response to an evident Iranian breach of the JCPOA.

3. Conduct contingency planning and exercises for operations to prevent Iran from acquiring a nuclear weapon.

4. Maintain a robust military presence in the Middle East.

5. Undermine Iranian asymmetric activities in the Middle East and around the world by publicizing them and using their exposure to embarrass and isolate Iran.

6. Dedicate more resources to identify and impede the Islamic Revolutionary Guard Corps' (IRGC) economic role at home and abroad.

7. Aggressively identify, sanction, and counter Iranian missile procurement activities.

8. Take military steps to ensure that Iran-supported militias and Hezbollah are kept out of the Golan Heights and southwestern Syria.

9. Dedicate more resources to aggressively identify and sanction leaders, businesses, bankers, and facilitators aiding Hezbollah's violent operations.

10. Limit a so-called land bridge from Iran to the Mediterranean by positioning U.S.-supported forces to retake most territory held by the self-proclaimed Islamic State in eastern Syria.

11. Prevent or limit a conventional Iranian military buildup in Syria.

12. Aggressively identify and sanction the individuals and entities Iran uses to support Syrian President Bashar al-Assad.

13. Maintain a small long-term military presence in Iraq at current force levels.

14. Posture military forces to clearly message Iran that any effort to disrupt the flow of trade through the Bab al-Mandeb strait will be met with firm U.S. resolve.

15. Engage in the close military and intelligence collaboration with Israel and other U.S. allies in the region on checking the most disconcerting aspects of Iranian activity.

16. Support targeted maritime interdiction operations to intercept Iranian arms shipments.

17. Continue military assistance to regional Gulf partners.

18. Proceed with care in addressing evidence that any Iranian entity de-listed under the JCPOA is conducting a sanctionable activity.

Since virtually the entire Western world fell prey to the illusion that the Iran deal is "the best we can do" to prevent Iran from building and using a nuke against us and our allies, there are practically no feasible options left anymore.

However, we can't give up because the agreement might slow down Iran's nuke development for some years. Since thcy Mullahs don't allow the IAEA to inspect their facilities freely (and military installations not at all), we can't even be sure of that. What's left is only maintaining

the pressure on Iran and hoping for an out-of-the-box
solution Donald Trump is so famous for.

How to practice Christian compassion

Compassion is a feeling of deep sympathy and sorrow for another who is hurting, in pain, or has misfortune and is accompanied by a strong desire to help the suffering people.

As much as we must fight ferociously against the deadly enemies of our Judeo-Christian heritage, we also must teach, live and practice Christian compassion for the poor, underprivileged as well as the politically and socially misfortunate in the world.

As the Bible proves, Jesus Christ is the greatest example of someone with true compassion. Not only did Jesus have compassion and heal people from physical suffering. He also showed the greatest compassion for mankind when died on the cross for our sins.

Christianity is absolutely unique. No other religion or philosophy values and practices indiscriminate taking care of the young, sick, orphaned, oppressed, and widowed. Christian humanitarian organizations work tirelessly around the world to spread hope, faith, and charity.

This is not new. Christian hospitals spread to Europe by the eighth century. By the mid-1500s, thirty-seven thousand Benedictine monasteries cared for the ill. Christianity was in the process changing the world, even beyond the West.

Existentially important also was the medical nursing, a Christian innovation in ancient times, took leaps forward through the influence of Christ-follower Florence Nightingale. In 1864, Red Cross founder Jean Henri Dunant confessed on his deathbed, "I am a disciple of Christ as in the first century, and nothing more."

This unique Christian attitude of charity and compassion continues today in Christian societies like the Salvation Army and other Christian groups who aided flood, fire or hurricane victims better than our government. Christian compassion is characterized best by the following three fundamental virtues:

1. Faith
2. Hope
3. Charity

As Christians, we all know that Christ is alive and can be served directly by serving those in the greatest need.

"For I was hungry, and you gave me something to eat; I was thirsty, and you gave me something to drink; I was a stranger, and you invited me in" (Matthew 25:35).

How to help the helpless

We all want to help those in need, but it can be sometimes confusing and somewhat overwhelming to choose which charity will do the most good.

All Christian-based charities listed here were chosen based on several key criteria areas and verified by top charity watchdog groups, such as Charity Navigator, GuideStar, and Ministry Watch. They also were evaluated for being transparent in their financial reporting, accountable for the distribution of all donations received, having recently and regularly filed IRS 990 tax forms, maintaining a low percentage of operating costs, and demonstrating a high percentage of donations going directly to the needy. They all need and deserve our donations:

1. Samaritan's Purse
2. Compassion International

3. Lutheran World Relief
4. Operating Blessing International
5. Advancing Native Missions
6. Children's Hunger Fund
7. Salvation Army
8. Catholic Relief Services
9. Lifeline Christian Mission
10. Food for the Poor

There is a lot of information about these charities available online. Inform yourself thoroughly before you get involved and select the charity you want to support with your donation. Here is how you might want to begin:

1. Begin in your own church and go from there
2. Look for simple, practical and effective ways to help
3. Involve experts you can trust
4. Be aware that spiritual problems require spiritual solutions
5. Pray and trust God for the results

How to help the persecuted Christians

Christian persecution has a long history. It started in the first century when Romans tried to eradicate the early church in the Middle East. Then, countless other political and religious forces fought brutally against the idea of Christianity, differing philosophically, morally and religiously from all other competing cultural and religious influences.

Muhammad's invention of Islam in the seventh century created a new life-and-death enemy for Christians all over the world. A short glance at Koran's Sharia law proves that Christianity and Islam are absolutely incompatible.

While the Christian Bible proclaims light, love, and forgiveness, Muslims cherish darkness, intolerance and deadly vengeance against all infidels.

Therefore, there is no accident that Christians face the deadliest persecution in all Muslim countries. Despite daily proof and cruel documentation, the UN and virtually the entire West disregarded the dire problem entirely.

The actual situation is much worse than most people know or can imagine. Open Doors published specific numbers allowing us to comprehend the seriousness of the catastrophe:

1. Approximately 215 million Christians experience high, very high, or extreme persecution.

2. North Korea remains the most dangerous place to be a Christian (for 14 straight years).

3. Islamic extremism remains the global dominant driver of persecution, responsible for initiating oppression and conflict in 35 out of the 50 countries on the 2017 list.

4. Ethnic nationalism is fast becoming a major driver of persecution. "While this took an anti-establishment form in the West, in Asia it took an anti-minorities form, fueled by dramatic religious nationalism and government insecurity. It is common—and easy—for tottering governments to gain quick support by scapegoating Christians."

5. The total number of persecution incidents in the top 50 most dangerous countries increased, revealing the persecution of Christians worldwide as a rising trend.

6. The most violent: Pakistan, which rose to No. 4 on the list for a level of violence "exceeding even northern Nigeria."

7. The killings of Christians in Nigeria saw an increase of more than 62 percent.

8. The killings of Christians were more geographically dispersed than in most time periods studied. "Hitting closer to home, 23 Christian leaders in Mexico and four in Colombia were killed specifically for their faith," said Open Doors of the "rare" event.

9. The worst increase: Mali, which moved up the most places on the list from No. 44 to No. 32.

10. Asia is a new center of concern, with persecution rising sharply in Bangladesh, Laos, and Bhutan, and Sri Lanka joining the list for the first time.

Most help for terribly oppressed Christians in the Middle East, Asia, and other places comes from private Christian charities such as Open Doors or Billy Graham Ministry.

Their work is highly impressive and terribly needed. For over 60 years, Open Doors has worked in the world's most oppressive countries, empowering Christians who are persecuted for their beliefs.

Open Doors equips persecuted Christians in more than 60 countries through programs like Bible & Gospel Development, Women & Children Advancement, and Christian Community Restoration.

It is not a coincidence that almost all countries persecuting Christians are governed by a Muslim regime. The Islamist movement is "the part of Islam which embraces a clear political agenda for bringing nations under Muslim domination and Sharia law," Open Doors states.

The effect is mind-boggling: "Every day six women are raped, sexually harassed, or forced into marriage to a Muslim under threat of death due to their Christian faith," Open Doors reports. Actually, this number is likely very low, since it includes only officially reported incidents.

What can we do? You are not as helpless as you might think.

1. Join Christian organizations involved
2. Donate funds to help with their work
3. Become activist for Christian faith
4. Organize activist groups
5. Collect facts and general information
6. Make media aware of the facts
7. Use social media platforms
8. Contact Congressmen and Senators
9. Establish an activist group in your church
10. Pray for the persecuted Christians

How to start a spiritual renewal

Our daily life poses countless challenges and deflections from what is really important for our spiritual wellbeing. We are often overwhelmed with superficial actions, demands, and problems and don't realize what is "normal" anymore. Our daily pressures and lifestyle chaos sometimes become "the new normal", and we are doomed. We've lost it, and we sometimes even don't realize it.

Why is your peace of mind, your peace with God and your peace with your next ones so vital? You can get a complete answer in my book "Find peace of mind – or lose your mind", but here is a short answer: How can you fight for the survival of our humanity if you are spiritually "messed up" yourself?

The scriptures are always the answer to all spiritual questions we might have. Any kind of spiritual renewal must be based on the following principles:

1. We Christians must unify in our effort to improve the world
2. We Christians must start respecting God's word
3. We Christians must start understanding God's word
4. We Christians must start obeying God's word

Most people don't even recognize that they urgently need a spiritual renewal. Watch for indicators signaling your need to renew your spiritual life.

1. Do you start ignoring God's word?
2. Do you harbor hidden sins from the past?
3. Do you neglect your Christian responsibilities?
4. Do you deliberately disobey God?
5. Do you run away from God's calling?
6. Do you disregard God's corrections?

If you too need a spiritual renewal, don't hesitate, procrastinate and wait. You must act and find solutions to your spiritual problem. Here are some very important tips:

1. Let God help you
2. Start finding tranquility
3. Find peace with God, yourself and others
4. Receive God's forgiveness
5. Pray about your worries
6. Let God control your life
7. Don't compare yourself to others

8. Search for wisdom and counsel
9. Find transcendent peace
10. Go where peace is
11. See the invisible

You will discover that you can be a peaceful, God-loving and composed human being - and a determined political activist and warrior of the Judeo-Christian civilization at the same time.

Connect with like-minded people and organizations

In order to be an effective activist for traditional morals and values, you must be very outgoing, inventive and rhetorically savvy. The most important thing is spreading your message with all methods and tricks available. You must be a very good communicator!

First of all, you must do your homework and study every topic and aspect you intend to present. Never forget, there is a war of words, facts and clashing ideologies out there.

Fortunately, you have the biggest advantage available. Most facts support our worldview. We just have to present them effectively enough. However, this exactly is our biggest problem. As good as our facts and arguments are, most conservatives do a lousy job to present them effectively.

The left is by far superior in presenting their talking points. The reason is not just because the media is picking up their "version of the truth". It is because socialists are dialectically much smarter than us. The main reason is that they don't use virtually any facts (they mostly anyway don't have), they use emotions! And emotions are a much better seller than (boring) facts….

We must recognize that and adjust to their style or political war. We can't continue to fight with dull pocket knives, while socialists are slaughtering us with machetes….

We have the morals, we have the principles, and we have the facts. Now we must try to become like the "greatest communicator": Ronald Reagan who demonstrated his skills brilliantly.

The Conservative Policy Forum published a list of values defining conservatism.

1. Pro responsibility and self-reliance
2. Pro enterprise and free market
3. Pro personal freedom
4. Pro-defense
5. Pro-justice
6. Pro community
7. Pro opportunity
8. Pro compassion
9. Pro-democracy
10. Pro principles
11. Pro future

Here is a list of major conservative organizations in the US you might want to join, use or cooperate with:

Accuracy in the Media
Alliance Defending Freedom
American Center for Law and Justice
American Conservative Union
American Enterprise Institute
American Family Association
Association of American Physicians and Surgeons
Campus Reform
Cato Institute
Christian Coalition
Center for Immigration Studies
Center for Media Affairs
Club for Growth
CommonSense.org
Concerned Women for America
Conservative Policy Forum
Council of the Conservative Caucus
Eagle Forum
Family Research Council
Federation for American Immigration Reform

First Liberty Institute
Focus on the Family
Freedom Works
Gun Owners of America
Heritage Foundation
Home School Legal Defense Association
Hudson Institute
Leadership Institute
John Birch Society
Judicial Watch
Liberty Counsel
Manhattan Institute
Media Research Center
National Rifle Association
National Right to Life
National Right to Work Committee
Numbers USA
Susan B. Anthony List
Tea Party Patriots
Tenth Amendment Center
Traditional Values Coalition
Operation Rescue
Parents Television Council
The Federalist Society

Bill of Rights

The first ten Amendments to the US Constitution make up our Bill of Rights.

The First Amendment
provides that Congress make no law respecting an establishment of religion or prohibiting its free exercise. It protects freedom of speech, the press, assembly, and the right to petition the Government for a redress of grievances.

The Second Amendment
gives citizens the right to bear arms.

The Third Amendment
prohibits the government from quartering troops in private homes, a major grievance during the American Revolution.

The Fourth Amendment
protects citizens from unreasonable search and seizure. The government may not conduct any searches without a warrant, and such warrants must be issued by a judge and based on probable cause.

The Fifth Amendment
 provides that citizens not be subject to criminal prosecution and punishment without due process. Citizens may not be tried on the same set of facts twice, and are protected from self-incrimination (the right to remain silent). The amendment also establishes the power of eminent domain, ensuring that private property is not seized for public use without just compensation.

The Sixth Amendment
assures the right to a speedy trial by a jury of one's peers, to be informed of the crimes with which they are charged, and to confront the witnesses brought by the government. The amendment also provides the accused the right to compel testimony from witnesses, and to legal representation.

The Seventh Amendment
provides that civil cases also be tried by a jury.

The Eighth Amendment
prohibits excessive bail, excessive fines, and cruel and unusual punishments.

The Ninth Amendment
states that the list of rights enumerated in the Constitution is not exhaustive and that the people retain all rights not enumerated.

The Tenth Amendment
assigns all powers not delegated to the United States, or prohibited to the states, to either the states or to the people.

God

help

us!